A Fashion for Extravagance

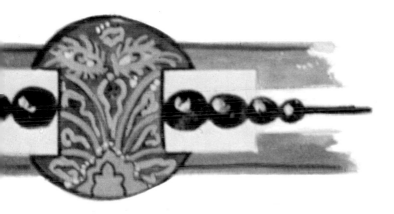

A FASHION FOR EXTRAVAGANCE

Art Deco Fabrics and Fashions

Sara Bowman

Michel Molinare

E. P. Dutton   New York

First published, 1985, in the United
States by E. P. Dutton
Text © Sara Bowman, 1985
Photographs © Michel Molinare,
1985 (except where otherwise
indicated)
All rights reserved.

Published in the United States by
E. P. Dutton, 2 Park Avenue,
New York, N.Y. 10016.

Library of Congress Catalog Card
Number: 85-71014

ISBN: 0-525-24358-5

Designed by Malcolm Harvey Young
Produced in Great Britain

CUSA

10 9 8 7 6 5 4 3 2 1
First Edition

To my mother and father

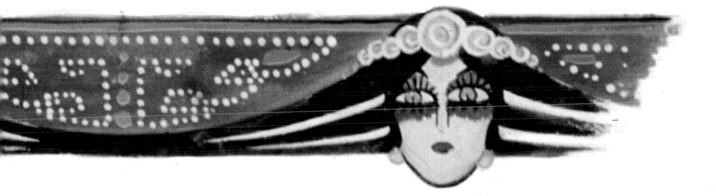

PREFACE

Ten years ago I was in Paris visiting Madame Poiret, the widow of the great couturier Paul Poiret. As I entered Madame Poiret's apartment in Rue Washington, a remarkable woman called Suzanne Lallement was taking her leave, and it was from this chance meeting that I discovered the embroideries that form the inspiration for this book.

Suzanne Lallement invited me to her home in Avenue Wagram, located above a baker's shop. It was a large and gracious apartment, full of beautiful things, indeed a treasure trove. Stored in cardboard boxes was a unique collection of sumptuous embroideries and sample books, which she had had the foresight to preserve when her family's famous embroidery house 'La Maison Lallement' closed in 1950. Poiret, Chanel, Callot, Doucet and all the other main couturiers had used these embroideries in their collections.

Suzanne Lallement, like so many of her friends, had been a craftswoman since the twenties and had executed exclusive embroideries and silks for haute couture. Now in their eighties these talented needlewomen and artists continued working. She introduced me to her circle of friends including Sonia Delaunay the painter, Aia Bertrand from the Duncan Academy, Arletty, Alice Natter from the Atelier Martine, Margarette Gallot, Jean Dorville and Ugo Lo Monaco — all of them inspiring artists.

As an Australian brought up to celebrate and respect European craft traditions I found the unique quality of their work immediately apparent. What surprised me constantly was that it was still so little known to the world at large. This can be explained partly by the fact that until recently craft in general, and embroidery and textile art in particular, have had a low status in the public eye. Also, embroidery work is, to a great extent, practised by women working from their homes, and is often hidden away and unrecognized.

Michel Molinare and I worked together photographing and documenting the lives and work of these people who were some of the few living contacts with the world of Parisian haute couture in the 1920s. We discovered rare and fascinating textile collections as well as the sketches and working drawings that lay behind them. *A Fashion for Extravagance* gives an insight into the background behind some of the outstanding new directions in design that took place in the early part of this century and forms a tribute to some of the artists who contributed to the Art Deco style.

CONTENTS

INTRODUCTION

By the turn of the century, Paris had become the most important artistic capital in the world, attracting artists from all over Europe and America. These artists, stimulated by the dynamism of a rapidly changing world, challenged academic traditions and broke away from conventional art forms, initiating the new modern art movements of Fauvism, Cubism, Dadaism, Futurism and Surrealism. At the same time, art and fashion became more clearly and closely related, each complementing and influencing the other.

Paris was the arbiter of fashion and the home of haute couture which had first been established there by Charles Worth in the 1850s. By 1900 it was an important and expanding industry, and between then and 1920 over twenty new houses were established, many of which were run by women. These Maisons de la Couture were magnificent establishments, many of them in former palaces. Twice a year, in the spring and summer, fashionable women flocked to Paris for the collections shown by individual houses in sparsely furnished salons adorned with gilt mirrors and thick pile carpets, to select their extensive wardrobe – day dress, motoring dress, afternoon dress, cocktail dress or evening dress, together with all the necessary accessories. Mrs de Acostia Lydwig, an American millionairess, was a client of La Maison Callot Soeurs. Indeed, she virtually supported the house. Her wardrobe included 'jackets and coats made of rich and rare materials worn with velvet skirts by day, or satin culottes for evening, black lace mantillas as light as gossamer ... blouses of embroidered batiste needlework or bobbin lace ... cobweb thin stockings with rare lace insertions and rose point petticoats.'

Fashion, which had been an aristocratic prerogative, now became available to whoever could afford the exorbitant prices of original and exclusively designed dress. High fashion clothes were all made from the finest silks, satins and brocades lined with silk and hand finished, so fashionable women needed generous dress allowances. The cost of a single couture dress in 1900 could be more than a seamstress earned a year. In New York in 1900, a skilled seamstress earned ten dollars for working an eighty-four hour week. In France the specialist craft workshops who made all the embroideries, lace, trimmings and artificial flowers for haute couture, depended on a large network of low paid homeworkers in Paris and the provinces.

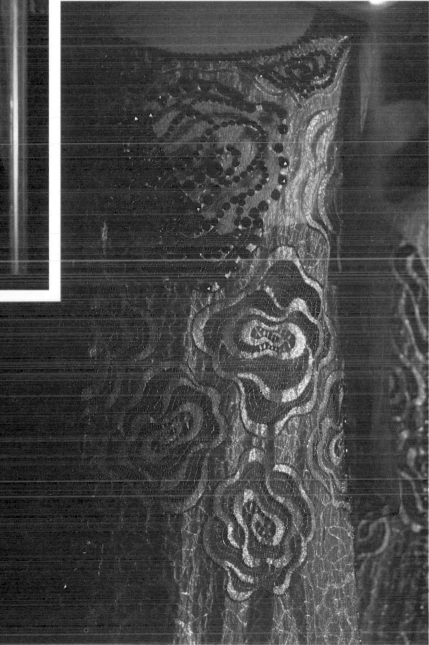

Below: Evening dress overlaid with metallic lace and hand beaded. The beading, sewn onto fragile fabrics, could weigh as much as 9lbs and helped dresses to fall in the straight, tubular fashion characteristic of the 1920s.

Above: A typical sumptuously embroidered dress, worked in metallic gold thread, embellished with beads, hand sewn onto a fine red chiffon ground. The practice of beading extensively onto fragile fabrics explains why so few of these dresses have survived.

In 1909, Serge Diaghilev, the great Russian impressario, presented for the first time the sensational Ballet Russe. Its influence on art and fashion was great and long lasting. The exotic costumes and sets, designed by Leon Bakst, with bold bright colours and designs, the sumptuous fabrics and embroideries, and the decorative splendour of the ballet *Scheherazade* had an enthusiastic audience, and an immediate appeal to designers and artists. The originality of the production, the music by Rimsky Korsakov, the sets by Bakst, the choreography by Fokine, and the supremacy of the dancers took Paris by storm. Orientalism became the order of the day for fashion and interiors and its influence firmly stamped the developing Art Deco style.

Art Deco, which made its appearance before the First World War, was a new style with an emphasis on surface decoration. In particular it made use of lush floral and oriental designs based on eighteenth century craft traditions. After the War, designs became more angular and geometric, following the lead of the Cubist and Futurist movements.

The Art Deco style was ideally suited to textile design. Dresses were extravagantly decorated, many with fantastic designs closely allied to contemporary painting, which were executed by skilled

A wedding dress made from a silk shift overlaid with metallic lace, which is carried on over the immensely long train displayed alongside it.

Women working in an embroidery workshop in the 1920s using wooden stretchers to hold the fabric taut. As was not uncommon, several women are working simultaneously on a single dress length, but even so it could take up to three weeks to bead a complete dress.

craftsmen working in textile ateliers. As in the days of the royal courts when artists were commissioned to create dress and textiles, so again in Paris in the early twentieth century artists and craftsmen worked together in the field of haute couture to achieve outstanding results. Paul Poiret, the great couturier, working between 1903 and 1930, set the precedent for others, becoming a veritable prince of patrons — commissioning young artists to work for him on everything from textiles and fashion to interior and theatre design. Some artists like Sonia Delaunay, Mariano Fortuny and Raymond Duncan set up their own textile printing workshops, where they applied their art to dress and fabrics. Others, like Cocteau, Léger, Picasso and Matisse, collaborated on theatrical productions, creating sensational costumes and set designs. Artists like Raoul Dufy and Jean Dorville designed stunning embroideries, silks and other fashion fabrics.

The First World War brought radical changes to women's lives. Many had taken an active part in the war effort, and afterwards they continued working. Couturiers responded to the demands of the newly emancipated woman by creating a tubular and loose dress which was easy to wear. Developments in communications, cinema news-reels and an increased number of fashion magazines ensured that women were well informed about fashion changes. Through mass produced dress fashion became accessible and available to all.

Couture dress, however, was distinguishable by its exclusivity in design and quality of finish. During the twenties, the originality of a dress often depended on the couturier's use of exclusively designed fabrics, embroideries, trimmings, pleating and shirring, which were used inventively to create decorative details.

The initial post-War shortage of heavy woollen cloth ensured the immediate acceptance of the softer line favoured by Poiret before the War. Technical developments within the textile industry by the 1920s meant that a variety of new and exciting fabrics, including artificial silk, were already available. These were an important and constant source of influence and inspiration to the couturier. Fabrics were used in startling and unusual combinations to emphasize texture – lamés were overlaid with cobweb-thin metallic lace, silks and velvets were printed and painted with angular and geometric designs and Cubist, Futurist, Egyptian and African motifs were used decoratively. The most extravagant fabrics were reserved for evening dress, however, and were used in startling colour combinations. 'Gold and silver brocade, with designs stamped in green velvet, silver and gold cloth with crystal embroidery, leaf green lamé with salmon tafetta, pink moirée and cloth of gold, hyacinth blue and gold brocade.'

After the War, the fashionable indulged in extravagant living. Dancing became the rage – even during lavish dinners guests danced such steps as the tango and black bottom between courses. Jazz clubs and tea dances multiplied, and the rigid pre-War society

Two mannequins with stylized cloth faces. These were used to display embroidered fashion accessories for sale. The one on the right represents Mistinguett, a famous cabaret singer of the 1920s.

JEAN DORVILLE

An illustration from Jean Dorville's *Poème Mécanique*, an avant garde theatrical production with slides, much acclaimed by Jean Cocteau and others. This design is typical of the ideas Dorville was experimenting with during this period. Like many artists, he applied his talents to fields such as theatre design and haute couture as well as to fine art.

changed to accommodate the new monied classes. One of the most fashionable night spots was *Le Boeuf Sur le Toit* in Rue Boissy d'Anglais, a cabaret named after one of Jean Cocteau's farces, which was run by Louis Moyses. 'Here, "chic" talent, renowned beauty and vice had the market value of a landed title. Chic enthroned Chanel where Poiret had never been accepted as a social equal by the women he dressed – talent and renown sanctified Derain, Picasso, Artur Rubinstein, Farque, Satie. Beauty admitted names which did not outlive their faces – but vice threw the doors open.'

'Those New Year's Eve galas at the Boeuf,' were recalled by the poet Blaise Cendrars. 'Clement Doucet and Jean Wiener would play endlessly on back-to-back pianos. On entering I knew whom I would meet there. There was that seaworthy dowager, the old Duchess d'Uzès, with her straight talk, her clay pipe, her bottle of Bordeaux. There was Coco Chanel, a loner. When the jazz warmed up, Jean Cocteau, like a jack-o'-lantern, his wick smelling of heresy, would perch himself behind the drums. There was Marthe Chenal trying once again to get her grappling hooks into Ambroise Vollard, that white Negro, by making him dance. There was the publisher Peignot, who, one Christmas night, after leaving Le Boeuf drove his car down the steps of the Madeleine Métro station, then came back up in reverse. There was Madame Leygues, with her famous necklace of I don't remember how many, many meters of pearls, Misia Sert, young Auric, old Fargue...'

The International Exhibition of Decorative Arts and Industry opened in Paris in 1925. It was originally intended to take place before the War and was conceived as a showcase for French craftsmanship. The Exhibition's pavilions were situated between the Grand and Petit Palais and boutiques were built along the linking bridges of the Seine. The Pavillon de Lyons celebrated the work of the French textile industry, and included magnificent silks designed by Raoul Dufy for Bianchini-Férier. The Pavillon d'Elegance, decorated by Jeanne Lanvin, showed work of over 60 couturiers displayed on stylized models designed especially by Vigneau Siégal. Paul Poiret chose to show his work separately on three barges which he moored on the Seine. Mariano Fortuny's intricate fabrics and timeless Delphos dresses were to be seen in the Italian section and Raymond Duncan displayed his silks and paintings too. Sonia Delaunay – pointing the way to new design directions – showed her simultaneous dress and fabrics at the Boutique Simultanée.

The splendour of the Art Deco style was epitomized at this International Exhibition. It was a style in which artists and artisans collaborated to achieve outstanding and lasting results.

POIRET

Paul Poiret, the French couturier, was not only an original artist of dress, he was also a great innovator in many related fields including fashion photography, fashion illustration, interior decoration, textile design and the luxury goods industry. He was the first couturier to create his own perfume house – Rosine.

Poiret was a man of his time, a man of extravagance, which was reflected in all aspects of his life and work. The son of a Parisian cloth merchant, he was born in Paris in 1879 and despite expressing an interest in fashion at an early age he was apprenticed to an umbrella maker. However he still managed to find the time to design dress, the first of which he sold to Madame Chéruit, a leading couture house. Doucet, the most fashionable and influential couturier at this time, recognized his talent and invited him to join his house. This Poiret did, working as an under tailor and acquiring valuable skills.

Doucet dressed many theatrical personalities and he invited Poiret to create some costumes for Réjane, and later for Sarah Bernhardt in her title role in Rostand's *L'Aiglon*. Uninvited Poiret, together with a friend, watched the rehearsal and voiced his disappointment with her acting skills. She complained to Doucet, and Poiret was dismissed with three months' pay.

This was the incentive Poiret needed. After a short spell working for Worth, he opened his own house at 5, Rue Auber in 1903 when he was just twenty-five years old. With limited capital and the assistance of eight seamstresses, Poiret's was soon to become one of the most fashionable and avant garde establishments in Paris. To draw attention to his new venture, he created startling window displays which he changed twice a week. They soon became the talking point amongst the fashionable.

Influenced by classical antiquity and the work of Nattier and Ingres, Poiret created a revolution in dress by dispensing with the S-shaped corset. Replacing it with a straight girdle he introduced a new slim line that was to become characteristic of twentieth century fashion. Not content with this alone, he introduced a palette of fauvist colours and commissioned artist friends to design his own textiles. He set up a school of decorative arts called Martine, which later became an interior design house, the Atelier Martine, creating and supplying fabrics and embroideries for the home.

A scene at the 1002nd Night party given by Poiret on 24 June 1911. (Collection de Wilde-Poiret)

Poiret, like Doucet, was a great patron of the arts and formed an extensive modern collection, including the work of Brancusi, Marie Laurencin, Derain, Dufy and Dunoyer de Segonzac. He brought artists together to collaborate on joint projects.

By 1909, Poiret's was the leading fashion establishment in Paris. He moved to larger premises in the Avenue d'Antin, in a magnificent eighteenth century mansion which had gracious rooms and large, well kept grounds. He commissioned Louis Suë, the architect, to adapt it to his requirements. The houses at the back, page houses for Louis XVI, became work rooms and living quarters for Poiret's family and he showed his collections in three adjoining rooms, which opened onto the garden. His spacious salon was carpeted in cherry red, and hung with large gilt mirrors, which reflected his luxurious creations.

To publicize his new ideas about fashion and new collections, Poiret gave magnificent fêtes and sumptuous fancy dress parties similar to eighteenth century masquerades, in the grounds of his couture house. He wrote that, 'It was not enough to be lavish, it was necessary to be unique. Instead of putting out vast sums for publicity as did other businessmen of my day, I prefer to give a great celebration.'

One of the most magnificent and splendid celebrations Poiret gave was the 1002nd Night given to publicize his excitement and interest in the Orient. Great attention was paid to detail — Raoul Dufy was appointed master of ceremonies and decoration, and together with de Segonzac he created magnificent oriental scenes and awnings. De Segonzac described it as follows: 'Dufy and I were

Opposite: Paul Poiret and his wife Denise, dressed as a Persian sultan and his favourite from the harem, for the 1002nd Night party. (Collection de Wilde-Poiret)

commissioned to paint an immense awning covering the entrance court, and representing Poiret as a turbaned sultan, sitting half-naked like a Buddha, with a flower in his hand. This vast painting was more than 100 square metres.'

The figure of Poiret was, 'gilded in the centre of a starry sky, surrounded by a wide border of magnificent flowers, painted in Dufy's characteristic manner.'

No expense was spared to conjure up the feeling of oriental splendour. The grounds were covered with oriental carpets; there was an oriental market, there were fire eaters, negro slaves served drinks and pink flamingoes ran loose in the garden. The great tragedian de Max recited verse from *The 1001 Nights*. Guests were requested to wear oriental attire – a doorman assessed their worth, and those whose clothes were not considered good enough were asked to change into other costumes provided. One guest for instance, despite the fact that he was wearing an original eighteenth century Chinese tunic, was asked to change as it was not Persian costume. Poiret, dressed as a sultan, was seated on a throne and his wife dressed as 'the favourite' was enclosed in a large gold cage with members of the harem. When the gates were flung open she stepped out, wearing harem trousers and a beautiful hooped skirt.

As a result of the 1002nd Night party Poiret was besieged with orders for his lampshade skirts, harem trousers and oriental embroideries. (Later, ironically, the man who had thus liberated fashion was to introduce the narrow, restrictive hobbled skirt.)

Poiret always cut a striking figure himself, and, using Max Jacob as his adviser, he dressed in loose oriental brocade jackets, tied with wide belts. Great attention was paid to the detail of his dress, his patent shoes were stamped with his monogram – PP – and he wore cuff-links with astrological devices, which were changed daily. He drove a large ivory coloured Renault, and was a distinctive figure at the races or with his models on his Grand Tour of Eastern Europe or the United States.

Poiret was an artist and original thinker. Through his many ventures, he brought new initiatives to the field of fashion illustration, inviting artists to make printed individual books of his designs, such as *Les Robes de Paul Poiret* by Paul Iribe. A second album, *Les Choses de Paul Poiret* was by George Lepape. The success of these prompted Lucien Voguel to set up the luxury journal *Gazette du Bon Ton*, which was a forum for new fashion ideas and fashion illustration where artists were invited to copy and interpret the work of the designer. Issues contained some of the most inventive and imaginative fashion illustrations of the twentieth century. Edward Steichen was commissioned to take fashion photographs (a new and successful departure) and Poiret styled the sittings personally. He established his own perfume house, Rosine, named after one of his daughters, and at a stroke initiated the luxury goods industry – which continues to provide much needed revenue to the individual couture houses.

After a trip to the United States in 1913 to promote his work,

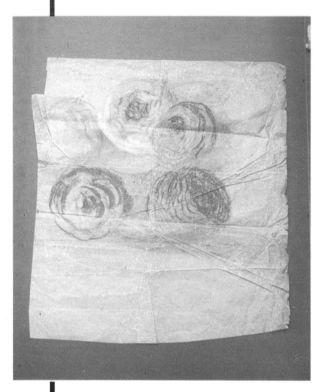

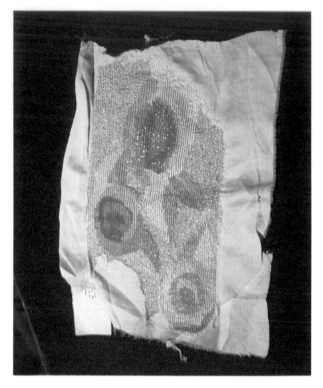

Above left: Working drawing on tracing paper, sketched with pastels.

Above right: Embroidered sample by Felix Lallement, in which the basic idea in the drawn sketch has been altered and developed slightly. The piece shows an inventive combination of machine and hand embroidery, worked with silk and metallic threads on a silk ground.

Right: Fashion plate from *La Gazette du Bon Ton* of a Poiret tunic incorporating a similar embroidered design.

Opposite: Poiret's 'Sorbet' design in satin and silk chiffon (1912) showing the glass bead embroidery used for the wired lampshade tunic shape that he introduced at the 1002nd Night party. (Photograph: Victoria and Albert Museum).

Evening coat entirely
hand beaded in tones of grey
gradually deepening into
black, and trimmed with
midnight blue velvet. The
coat dates from 1922 and
forms part of Souki Tomas's
extensive collection of haute
couture.

Detail of the beading of
the coat.

A group of Poiret's models in clothes designed by him, photographed in his garden in 1911. The picture is from a film called *L'Illustration* which he used to illustrate the numerous lectures he gave explaining his highly individual ideas on fashion. (Collection de Wilde Poiret)

Poiret saw copies of his designs in famous stores and quickly recognized the need for copyright legislation. He helped to set up Le Syndicat de Défense de la Grande Couture Française with Jacques Worth at its head. The war put a stop to its development however and it was not until the 1950s that legislation was passed.

At the International Exhibition of Decorative Arts in Paris in 1925 Poiret was not content with showing with the other couturiers. He moored three barges – Amours, Delices and Orgues – on the Seine, devoting one to the Atelier Martine, one to fashion, and one, a superb restaurant, to gastronomics. On 'Amours', the barge dedicated to Martine, Poiret could be seen behind a small piano. As each key was pressed, it released Rosine perfume. Unfortunately the lack of de luxe clients, many of whom had left Paris for the summer months, coupled with the changing feeling in design, was such that the barges ran at a great loss. Poiret was forced to sell his entire collection of paintings, which only covered the cost of half a barge.

Unable to assimilate the changes in society and among women themselves that were brought about by the Great War, Poiret continued designing for pre-war extravagance. During the early 1920s he opened 'The Oasis', a nightclub under a huge inflatable dome, but the trend for modern jazz clubs soon superceded it.

Between 1925 and 1929, Poiret's fashion house was in severe financial difficulties, and it was taken over and run by a board of directors. In 1929 it went into liquidation. During the 1930s he tried unsuccessfully to make a comeback.

Poiret, the father of modern fashion, was a man of vision and integrity. Unable to compromise with the commercial world, he became a painter to make a living and died in 1944.

MARTINE

An advertisement for fabrics from the Martine interior design house. Their designs became so fashionable that they opened a shop in Baker Street in London as well as their boutique in the Faubourg Saint-Honoré in Paris.

In 1911, Paul Poiret opened a school of decorative arts in Paris. He named it Martine after one of his daughters, (just as he had named his perfume Rosine after another daughter). Although the Martine school was short-lived, it instilled new life into the French decorative arts.

Poiret's decision to start the school was inspired by his enthusiasm for the new developments in the decorative arts in Vienna and Germany, particularly the work of Joseff Hoffmann and Bruno Paul. As well as his interest in the peasant arts and craft, which he had seen in Eastern Europe, Poiret 'dreamt of creating in France a movement of ideas that should be capable of propagating a new mode in decoration and furnishing.'

The school was based at 'La Maison Poiret', in the Avenue d'Antin, where Poiret set aside several rooms for the workshops. The members of the school were young 12 to 15 year old working class girls, who had just finished their schooling.

One student was Alice Ruty (later Natter) who was the fifth to join the school. A concièrge's daughter, she was in the habit of drawing with chalks on the pavement outside the apartment block where she lived. A friend of Poiret's saw these drawings and mentioned them to him. He subsequently enrolled her in his school. She became a prolific designer for the Atelier Martine and even later in her life, at 85 years old, when I met her, she was still working in this idiom, designing and making embroideries.

Although he was excited by the art schools in Vienna, Poiret was very critical of the way professors influenced and controlled students' designs. 'They were made to fit into a mould like an iron corselet.' He encouraged his students to work freely from nature. Initially he employed the wife of the painter Paul Seruzier to assist in the classes, but he soon found out that the students worked more creatively without artistic supervision.

Poiret's role, in his words, was 'to stimulate students' activity and taste without influencing them or criticising, so that the source of their inspirations should be kept pure and intact ... Whenever possible (he) had them taken into the country, or to the zoological gardens, or into conservatories, where each would do a picture according to whatever motive pleased her best. They used to bring back the most charming work. There would be fields of ripe corn, starred with marguerites, poppies and cornflowers; there were baskets of begonias; masses of hortensias, virgin forests through which sped leaping tigers, all done with an untamed naturalness that I wish I could describe in words', he said. 'I have pages of touching inspiration which sometimes approached the prettiest picture of the douanier Rousseau.'

From these designs, executed in bold bright colours in gouache, and pastels, Poiret selected a range suitable for reproduction. 'Then it was necessary for me to have the commercial courage, sometimes at great expense, to put into effect these daring incubations whose value might be misunderstood by the public.'

These designs were applied to fabrics for fashion, furnishings, wallpapers, ceramics, carpets, embroidery and mural decoration. Similar designs were used for interiors as well as fabrics and fashion. The girls wove their own designs for carpets and rugs and they also printed or embroidered their own fabrics.

The response to the work of the Martine school amongst art circles was excellent, and it was quickly recognized as a new direction in design. In 1912 an exhibition of their designs and their fabrics was put on at the Salon d'Automne.

The demand for Martine designs was such that Poiret opened a retail outlet called the Atelier Martine, at 83 Fauborg St Honoré, where a whole range of Martine designs were available – fabrics, curtains, embroidered cushions, glass, ceramics, hand-painted screens and furniture. *Vogue*, reviewing the shop in 1912, commented that there was 'everything that one could wish, and each article of the loveliest kind.' The Martines also used their designs to create magnificent mural decorations transforming shops, offices, tearooms, hotels, and private houses into exotic jungles and

Right: Alice Natter, photographed in her eighties. When she was a very young girl she was recruited as the fifth member of the Atelier Martine, and she continued working in the distinctive Martine style until her death.

Below: Some of Alice Natter's more recent cushion designs, still characterized by the bright bold design that was the Martine hallmark in the 1910s and 20s. They are worked on velvet grounds with a free and imaginative combination of yarns and fabrics.

The bedroom on the barge *Amours* in 1925, complete with Martine furnishings, fabrics, carpets and frieze. Poiret used these lavishly decorated barges to display his most recent fashions.

oriental palaces. Poiret wrote that, 'in front of a bare wall four metres high, they set up their ladders and then traced out their design in its actual size.' They turned Isadora Duncan's studio into what she described as a 'veritable Circe's kingdom', complete with gilded mirrors which reflected the heavy blue velvet drapery.

Quickly the Martines established an international reputation and a shop was opened in London at number 15 Baker Street. It was soon renowned for its exciting window displays of complete interiors. A black and white dining room with blown glass in the shape of fantastic fruit; bathrooms featuring translucent green glass bathtubs painted with porpoises and sea weed, and black glass decorated with scarlet lobsters chasing sea anemonies.

A double page from a Martine workbook (about 1910) showing a typical use of strong colours and simple, stylized motifs. The design is by Alice Natter.

A sample based on the painted design, machine embroidered on crêpe de Chine. When they were worked on fabric the designs were interpreted by the embroiderer into forms that could then be applied to a dress front, or perhaps to a cushion or some other fashion or furnishing idea. This piece was embroidered by the Maison Lallement, who often embroidered Martine designs.

Above and above right:
Three experimental
designs from the Martine
workbook, painted in
gouache, typical of the Art
Deco style in their lush,
oriental flavour.

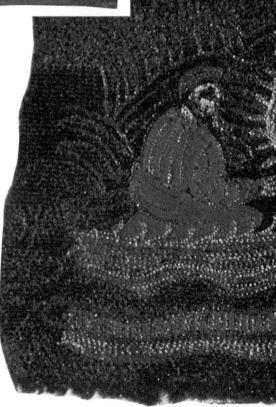

Right: An embroidery
sample made up from one of
the painted sketches machine
embroidered with metallic
thread. The piece of
embroidery would then have
been incorporated into one
of Poiret's designs, in this
case probably a dress fashion.

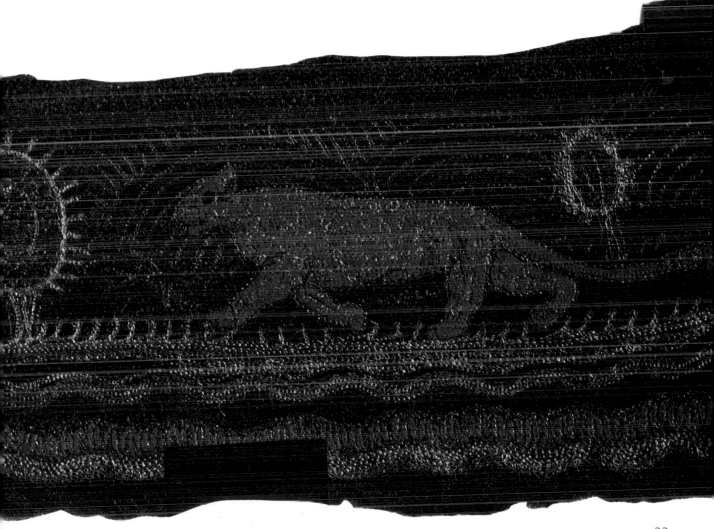

In 1914, the school closed for the duration of the war. Many of the girls were sent to Normandy, and were involved with ceramics and with teaching soldiers how to sew. At the International Exhibition of Decorative Arts in 1925, when Poiret moored his three barges on the Seine to display and publicize his work, the barge 'Amours' was transformed into a complete Martine interior. However, by 1925 design directions were already changing, and the demand for this style of work had passed its heyday.

This and the pictures that follow illustrate other working designs from the Atelier Martine. Poiret would encourage the girls to draw freely and would then select the ideas that could be best adapted for use as dresses, bags, belts, furnishing fabrics, cushions, wallpapers or carpets. The designs reflect the range of artistic thinking that was current in the fashion world at the time, while also sharing a bright, fresh spirit that was distinctively Martine.

Designs inspired by
Greek and Egyptian
antiquities were a popular
theme, and Poiret would
send the Martine girls on
visits to museums to gain
ideas which they would then
transform into something
altogether modern.

Three designs for round
carpets, typical of the
Martine style.

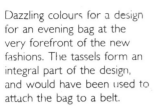

Dazzling colours for a design for an evening bag at the very forefront of the new fashions. The tassels form an integral part of the design, and would have been used to attach the bag to a belt.

Working drawings for
tassels which were a
recurrent feature of Poiret's
fashions.

A page from the Martine
workbook.

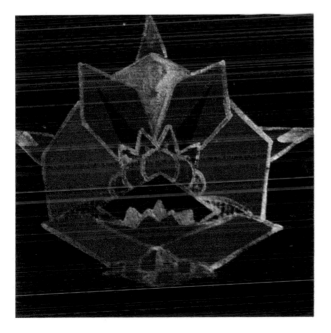

Sample of a Martine
fabric, hand beaded with jet
beads on a white velvet
ground.

43

A design probably
destined to become a
sumptuously elaborate
embroidery.

Design for a belt.

A double page from the
Martine workbook. Poiret
comments on the inspiration
his artists drew from nature:
'There would be fields of
ripe corn, starred with
marguerites, poppies and
cornflowers...'

DUFY

Some of the wood engravings for the days of the week designed by Dufy in 1910 as letter headings for Poiret. This was their first collaboration.

Raoul Dufy, the French painter renowned for his works illustrating the lives of the leisured class, is less well known for his sumptuous hand printed fabrics although he was one of the great innovators of twentieth century textile design. While working with Paul Poiret and later with Bianchini-Férier, (the leading French silk manufacturers between 1911 and 1930) he created a wealth of original Art Deco designs in silks, dress fabrics and wall hangings.

Dufy was one of a family of nine, and was born in Le Havre in 1877. When at school, he excelled at art but he left at fourteen to work for a Swiss importer of Brazilian coffee and had to continue his artistic studies at night school. In 1900, Dufy won a scholarship to the Beaux Arts in Paris, where he was a fellow student of Braque. He soon became part of the artistic circle of the period and was exposed to the work of Gauguin, Van Gogh, Pissaro, Monet and Matisse. In 1906, he exhibited at the Salon d'Automne with the Fauvists.

Like so many of his contemporaries his later experiments with cubism were not commercially successful, and in 1909 he was reduced to selling drawings to the Paris Journal for 5 francs a piece. At about this time, he was also involved with making woodblock prints as illustrations for a book of poems by Guillaume Apollinaire based on the *Bestiare d'Orphée*. He also produced individual prints such as *La Danse*, and *La Pêche*. When Poiret saw these prints he commissioned Dufy to design his personal stationery. The results were charming scenes, with a different woodcut for each day of the week, depicting scenes of daily life in the couture house. Wednesday depicted Poiret as a bearded gentleman, and Saturday, activities in the atelier. Dufy was later to assist in some decorative panels for Poiret's summer house together with huge awnings for Poiret's magnificent fêtes.

Dufy and Poiret shared similar visual fantasies, and a commitment to the decorative arts. Both were excited and also horrified by new developments in Vienna and Germany, especially L'Art Munichois which was the talk of Paris in 1910 when two complete floors were devoted to it at the Salon d'Automne. They also shared the same enthusiasm for the work of Poiret's newly founded school, the Ecole Martine and in 1911 they collaborated to initiate a new direction in textile design. In his autobiography *En Habillant l'Epoque* Poiret wrote of the beginnings of that venture:

'We had the same inclinations in decoration. His spontaneous and ardent genius had splashed with flowers the green panels of the doors of my dining room in the Pavillon du Butard. We dreamed of dazzling curtains, and gowns decorated à la Botticelli. Without counting the cost I gave Dufy, who was then making his beginnings in life, the means whereby to realize a few of his dreams. In a few weeks we fixed up a printing workshop in a little place in the Boulevard de Clichy, that I had specially hired. We discovered a chemist called Zifferlin, as tiresome as a bushel of fleas, but who knew from top to bottom all about the colouring matters, lithographic inks, aniline dyes, vats and acids. So here we were, Dufy and I, like Bouvard and Pecuchet, at the head of a new craft, from which we were about to draw new joys and exaltations.'

At the Petite Usine, or little factory, as it came to be called, Dufy experimented with block printing designs on to fabric. Poiret explained:

'Dufy drew for me and cut on wood, designs taken from the bestiary. From then on he created sumptuous stuffs, out of which I made dresses which have, I hope, never been destroyed. Somewhere there must be an amateur who has preserved these relics.'

The intricately hand-carved woodblocks were printed by hand in black outline onto grounds of silk, satin, linen, canvas or brocade. Further colours were applied with wooden sticks to achieve a hand-finished effect. Alice Ruty and her friend Agnes from the Martine school assisted sometimes with this work.

Dufy's fabrics' immediately aroused great interest. Poiret employed them extensively, creating magnificent coats, capes and dresses in sumptuous silk brocades block-printed with large designs, such as *La Perse* (see page 49). They were quite different from the available printed silk foulards which had small paisley or polka dot designs. Dufy's fabrics were stunning. When Poiret took his mannequins to the races to publicize them they were the centre of attraction.

Poiret also commissioned Dufy to execute a series of individual wall hangings, 2 metres square, based on woodcuts of *La Danse* and *La Chasse*. These were like tapestries, sharing the same border, and were to become prototypes for the large wall hangings Dufy made especially for Poiret and the Paris Exhibition in 1925.

Charles Bianchini, a partner in the leading French silk firm Bianchini-Férier based in Lyons, noticed the fabrics Dufy had created for Poiret, and recognized their commercial significance. He was to make Dufy one of the most influential twentieth century textile designers. Attempts by the firm to imitate Dufy's fabrics were unsuccessful, and so in 1911 Dufy was offered a contract. The silk manufacturers had offices in Paris, and Dufy was free to choose the style and quality of designs. Each week he went to the firm's

Dufy's fabric 'Les
Coquillages' made of silk
further decorated with silvery
metal lamé work.

Poiret evening dress made
from the Dufy fabric 'Les
Coquillages'. It was displayed
at the Exposition des Arts
Decoratifs, 1925.

Dufy's painting 'Roses et Feuillage' (1912–13) of a design for a printed silk in black and white. Flowers were one of Dufy's favourite themes for dress fabrics. In the early days he engraved the woodblocks and hand printed the fabrics himself. Particularly when he first worked with Poiret, he was intensely interested in cubist preoccupatons of form and design, and sought a very precise balance between areas of colour and space.

Poiret's evening cape 'La Perse' (1911), made from a printed Dufy velvet with a green silk lining and trimmed with fur. It was his friendship with Poiret that first gave Dufy the scope he needed to develop his talents. (Photograph: Helmut Newton)

PI.21 à 24.

Robes poi

A colour lithograph plate featured in *La Gazette du Bon Ton* 1920 of Dufy's 'Dresses for Summer'. The silk designs were for Bianchini-Férier.

offices in Avenue Opéra, where Charles Bianchini made his selection of designs based on their commercial viability. The designs he chose were carefully initialled and numbered, ready to be sent to the factory in Tournon, 50 miles south of Lyons, for production.

As Dufy no longer had time to carve the blocks, they were done by the company, Dournel. Dufy worked in association with Bianchini-Férier from 1911 to 1928, when he chose not to renew his contract and returned to his painting. Throughout the twenties he created original Art Deco silks, and many of his floral designs seemed as if they had been hand painted. He also created designs on woodblocks and in 1924 produced a series of silks using an eighteenth century style, with groups of figures performing different activities, surrounded by arabesques and foliage. Poiret continued to employ Dufy fabrics, and in 1920 an issue of *La Gazette du Bon Ton* featured Poiret's entire summer collection executed in Dufy's Bianchini-Férier silks.

They still continued to collaborate on joint artistic ventures. Dufy created huge wall hangings especially for Poiret which were made up of three horizontal bands of contrasting fabrics hand painted in white contour, with contemporary scenes such as the Admiral's party and Poiret's mannequins at the races. These were used to

L'été 1920.

Gazette du Bon Ton - N° 4 -

decorate one of Poiret's barges, Orgues, which was moored on the Seine to publicize his work for the Paris Exhibition.

After 1930, Dufy became totally involved with his painting and relegated his textile designing to a minor role.

The 'Cortège d'Orphée', a satin damasse designed for Bianchini-Férier in 1921. Greek themes were very prevalent at this time.

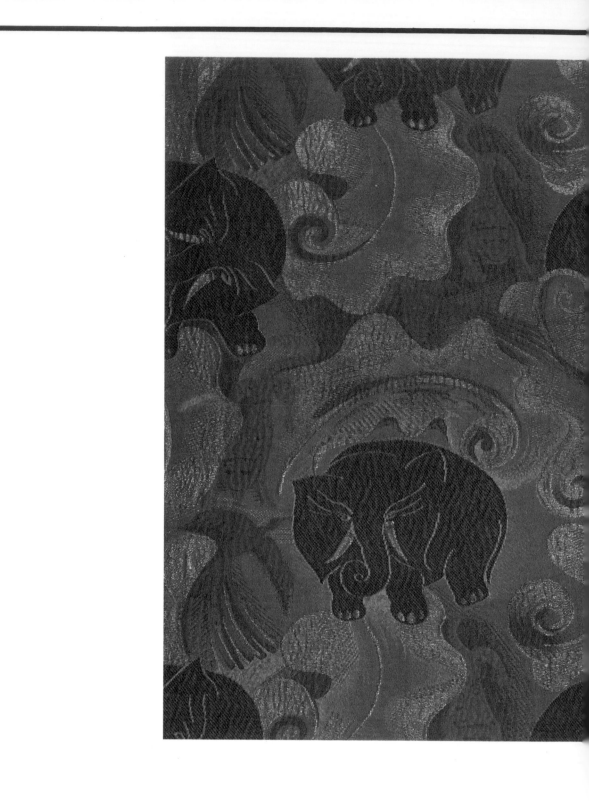

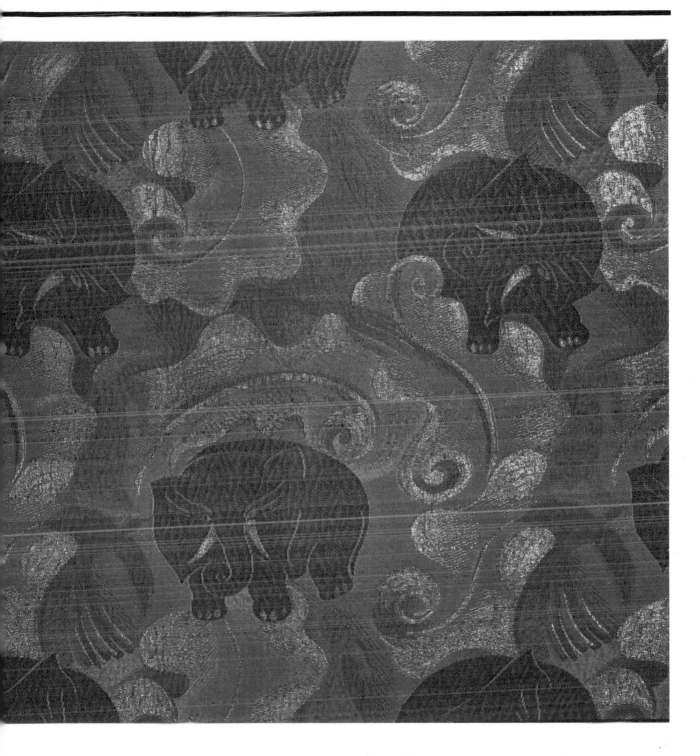

The 'l'Éléphant' panel from Dufy's *Bestiaire* collection of designs for the Bianchini-Férier factory in Tournon, featured in the fashion magazine *La Gazette du Bon Ton* in 1920. The design, comprised of black elephants with leopards and birds, worked on a crumpled rose material with gold threads and was also applied to green and blue satins. The design

Lithograph of a travelling coat by Dufy featured in *La Gazette du Bon Ton* in February 1920.

'Les Altheas' (1917).
These flamboyant floral
patterns were worked on a
mixture of printed and
woven fabrics for Bianchini-
Férier.

LA MAISON LALLEMENT

During the first quarter of this century, there was a resurgence of interest in embroidery. In 1900, Paris – the centre of haute couture – also became a centre for embroidery. The demand for exclusively designed and finely worked embroidery to decorate dress and furnishings led to an expansion in specialist workshops. By 1909 there were three thousand in Paris alone, and other fashion capitals such as New York, London and Hollywood supported a thriving industry.

The Art Deco style was ideally suited to embroidery, and by the 1920s it had reached a peak in design and workmanship. Embroidery was used extensively for fashion, both for day and evening wear. Even fashion accessories, hats, bags, gloves and shoes, were decorated with exclusive designs.

Specialist craft workshops staffed by superb craftspeople, designed and made all the intricate embroideries for haute couture. One of the most important houses was La Maison Lallement which was founded by Félix Lallement, and which supplied original hand and machine embroideries to the great couture houses between 1898 and 1950. Worth, Callot Soeurs, Doucet and Poiret commissioned their embroideries from him. Félix Lallement worked closely with Paul Poiret, executing the Martine designs, and creating sumptuous and splendid embroideries for dress.

At La Maison Lallement, three complete floors were reserved for hand and machine embroidery. Embroidery machines were used inventively. Although attachments were added to the electric Cornély embroidery machine for beading, tambour work proved more popular. (This was a method of applying beads by hand with a little hook.)

Embroidery was worked in a variety of techniques and materials: appliqué work, drawn thread work, metal clips, buttons, stencilling, leather appliqué work, raised cord, and even American cloth masquerading as patent leather. Specialist shops supplied a wide range of embroidery materials such as beads, pearls, studs, and gold and silver threads in 150 different widths and qualities, many imported from Japan. St Étienne, the centre of French ribbon production, supplied decorative ribbons, trimmings and gold and silver lace.

The embroidery workshops made two collections each year, of about 200 designs. Samples on fabric panels one foot square to

Suzanne Lallement, photographed in her seventies. She is the daughter of Félix Lallement, founder of the famous embroidery house, which she later took over and managed herself.

imitate the flat front of a dress, were shown to the individual couture houses who then selected designs and specified fabrics.

Embroidery was worked on a dress length supplied by the couturier with the dress pattern drawn out. Fabrics for embroidery were extravagant since only the finest were employed – silks, velvets, brocades, cloth of gold, georgette and silk chiffon. They were used in startling and unusual combinations to emphasize texture – fragile silks were combined with deep silk pile velvet, kasha cloth, chiffon, jersey and satin; gold and silver lamé were overlaid with cobweb-thin metallic lace.

In her book, *The Princess in Exile*, the Grand Duchess Maria of Russia described the specialist shops of the time in vivid detail:

'There was something decidedly stimulating to the imagination about the great warehouses where I bought my reels of china silk, wound up on large wooden spools. Heavy bales of raw silk stood around the floor, just as they had come from the Orient, with Chinese lettering on the coverings. The shelves were laden with the richest and most varied assortment of embroidery silks, all of which were of an exquisite quality. The place was flamboyant with colour; it was like moving through an enormous paint box, I loved fingering the silks and assembling and contrasting the shades.'

Day and evening dress was elaborately decorated. The tubular shape of the dress was an ideal surface for embroidery, and it was the most important feature of a dress. Mr Reville, the Queen's dressmaker writing in the *Embroideress* magazine of 1923 explained to his readers, 'that day as well as evening dress can now be embroidered without transgressing the laws of good dressing, and even fur can be embroidered without the wearer incurring the suspicion of vulgarity.' In 1922, *Vogue* reported that,

'every one who has seen the Paris collections, dwells on the beauty and novelty of the embroidery. Quite simple serge suits have the top part of the jacket covered with a mediaeval lattice of silver threads which Lanvin, for example, mingles with branches of coral. Daytime wraps of woollen fabrics startle us by having their entire back embroidered in large motifs, sometimes with appliqué in metal, silver tissue or coloured silks. Martial et Armand show a cape of heavy wool velour, with a back cut into a bold pattern and placed over cloth of gold. In almost every collection, there are evening gowns of solid embroidery in beads, paillettes and gold and silver threads.'

The exotic oriental and lush floral designs popular before the war gave way by the early twenties to more angular geometrical forms – such as Cubist, Futurist and Egyptian motifs.

The embroidery designer was a creative artist. Félix Lallement was one of the most highly regarded of his day and won a first prize at the International Exhibition of Decorative Arts in Paris in 1925. He also invited practising painters such as Jean Dorville to design embroideries. These designs were usually presented as a

A photograph of Jean
Dorville taken in 1976.

coloured working drawing — some were detailed and to scale and others were drawn on pieces of brown paper in crayons, gouache or pastels together with samples indicating the fabrics, yarns and techniques to be used, which were sent to the workrooms to be copied. First a tracing was made of the design which was transferred with a wheel on to the fabric, and white pouncing powder was then rubbed into the perforated outline of the design. When the tracing was removed, the white outline was fixed with an alcohol spray, and the material was ready to be worked.

In the Lallement atelier, there were thirty highly experienced embroideresses some of whom had been trained by the house. During the 1920s the demand for highly skilled staff was such that Félix Lallement opened an embroidery school, where young girls could receive a training. Homeworkers in the provinces embroidered the orders for dresses. Hand embroidery was worked on wooden frames and entire dress lengths were hand beaded, each one taking several women three weeks to complete. The fragility of the fabrics, such as crêpe de Chine and the fine silks, was such that they were worked through vanishing muslin.

The Lallement house also designed and made fashion accessories, especially bags and belts. The artist Margarette Gallot made all the intricate handworked decorations for dress which were available from a boutique in the Rue de Petit Champs. Embroidery designs and samples for dress, bags and cushions were exported to America to be copied. This trade ceased with the Wall Street Crash in 1929. During the thirties there was less demand for fashion embroidery, and consequently many houses closed with the subsequent loss of craft skills. Suzanne Lallement and her mother, both highly skilled embroideresses, ran the house after the death of Félix in 1938 until it closed in 1955.

A design for a stage curtain by the painter Jean Dorville who collaborated closely with La Maison Lallement and created designs for them.

A painting by Jean Dorville for his *Poème Mécanique* (see photograph, page 17).

Sample panel for a dress
front made up by La Maison
Lallement featuring nautical
themes. It is hand
embroidered on a
combination of wool and silk
grounds.

Sample on a blue silk
ground. The little blue sailor
hats are appliquéd on and
then embroidered with silk
pompoms and the names of
various ports.

Dress front sample
worked on a crêpe de Chine
ground outlined with machine
embroidery in metallic
thread. It has silk appliqué
work and is studded with
metal.

A model wearing the
dress made up into its final
form.

Cushion designs for La Maison Lallement. There was great scope for inventive designs for cushions, which were frequently based on artists' sketches.

Page from a Martine
workbook of designs that
would later be worked as
embroideries by the Maison
Lallement.

Detail on a pocket
embroidered by the Maison
Lallement on a ground of
alternating strips of wool and
silk with appliqued flowers in
leather.

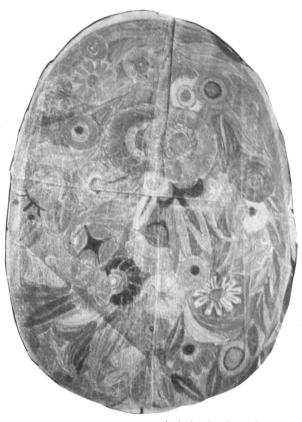

A design by the artist
Marguerite Gallot showing
floral themes typical of her
style. A painter in her own
right, she worked with La
Maison Lallement on designs
for fashion accessories.

Left: Marguerite Gallot,
photographed in later life.

Sketches for floral designs
created by the Atelier
Martine and then
embroidered by the Maison
Lallement.

Working drawing for an
embroidered design with
flying birds.

The magnificent dress panel that evolved from that design. Worked on a crêpe de Chine ground with gold and silver leather and orange wool appliqué work.

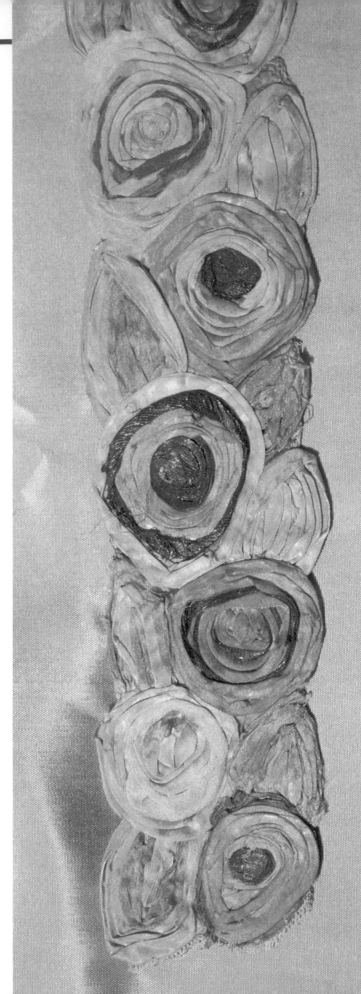

Original belt designed by
Marguerite Gallot made of
small pieces of silk taffeta
twisted into spiral rosettes
with silver lamé centres.

Painted design sketched in gouache on cartridge paper.

The taste for surface decoration was such that even a printed design would be further embellished with beadwork. This is a printed silk with a floral design on a hand beaded ground. The centres of the machine embroidered flowers are highlighted with silver thread.

A length of highly intricate embroidery on a gold and silver brocade, hand beaded with pearls and coloured glass stones. The piece was made for Poiret and the dress length probably took several weeks to bead.

A still of Hope Hampton taken from McCall's newsreel. The newsreels were used to show the latest fashions in Paris to American cinema audiences. The heavily beaded embroidery of this dress is typical of the time (1925).

A painted design for embroidery. Vivid full flowers such as these were a typical motif used extensively in textiles and other Art Deco arts.

Design for a bag in an oriental style, showing a seated man. The working drawing is coloured in on one side only, leaving the embroiderer to repeat the colours on the other half.

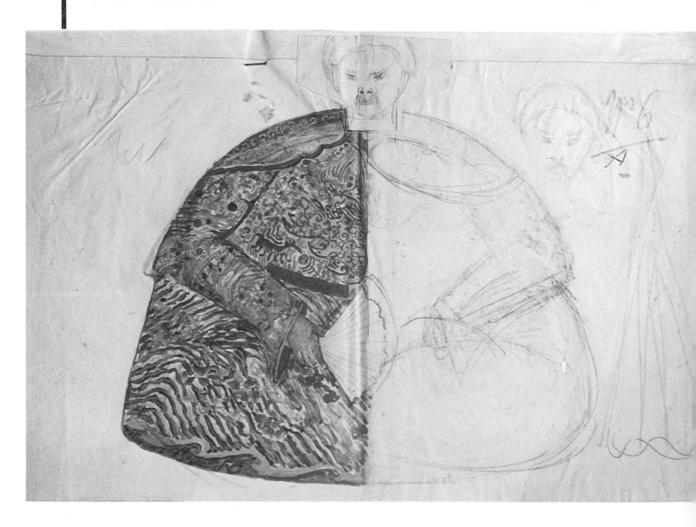

Artist's design for a bag.

A design with birds and fruit trees executed for La Maison Lallement.

A leather appliqué dress front design, on a ground which is a combination of black and ivory silk, with machine embroidery. These dramatic geometrical designs were an innovation of the Art Deco period. A typical Poiret tassel and evening bag are also shown.

Sample embroidery for a dress front, using another stylized bird design (compare the example on page 69). Worked on crêpe de Chine with braided appliqué.

The new energy in the theatre generated by the popularity of the Ballet Russe was reflected throughout the arts. This design on brown paper represents a character on stage holding a mask and a veil. There is a suggestion of curtains in the background and an onlooking oriental figure on the left. The design was probably intended for a cushion.

FORTUNY

Mariano Fortuny, the Magician of Venice, painter, inventor, theatre designer and photographer, is best known for his dress and textiles. Working outside the mainstream of haute couture, from the Palazzo Orfei in Venice, he created timeless dress variations on his original Delphos, precious original silks and rich velvets which were hand-painted and printed.

Mariano Fortuny was born in Granada, Spain in 1871 into a wealthy artistic family. His father, Mariano Fortuny y Marsal, was an artist of international standing. His untimely death in 1874 prompted the family to move to Paris to be in the company of Raymundo, his brother, who was a celebrated painter himself. They lived in an artistic, literary milieu and, encouraged by his mother, Mariano Fortuny developed an interest in the arts and himself became an accomplished painter and etcher. Later the family moved to Venice to the Palazzo Martinengo, where they settled.

Mariano Fortuny's private means enabled him to devote his time to painting and to pursuing his interests in the arts, photography, etching, lighting, interior decoration and theatre design. He worked in isolation. After his marriage in 1899, he moved out of the family home into the Palazzo Orfei, a magnificent thirteenth century palace built for the Pessaro family. He very quickly transformed it into something very much his own. A visitor described it:

'Last night I entered the mysterious Palazzo, and was spellbound by magic: I passed in front of lamps as bright as suns, and my body threw no shadows. I saw spread out on the walls of the immense rooms, enclosed in dazzling glass cases, many coloured hangings, brocades and damasks, of which not a thread was woven. I passed into a remote shut-up room, and saw the sky, a real sky, in calm and stormy weather, extending all round a vast amphitheatre.'

Like other artists of his day, Fortuny was interested in dress. His experience as a painter led him to use dress and drapery for his models that showed their natural beauty, and the shape of their body. Through designing theatrical costumes he became increasingly involved with designs and effects with cloth. This led to the creation of his famous Delphos dress which hung from the shoulders to the ground in finely pleated silks. It was named after

Fortuny's label which appeared on most of his clothes. His other form of labelling was to write his name on a piece of tape attached to the inside.

78

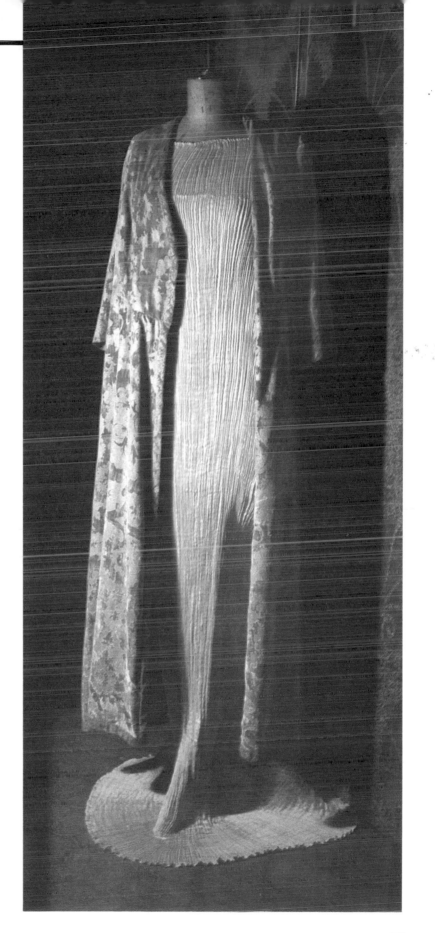

One of the many
variations on the Delphos
dress by Fortuny inspired by
the Ionic chiton. The secret
of how he created his
distinctive pleats remains an
unsolved mystery.

The Delphos dresses
were made of the highest
quality hand dyed silk
imported from Japan,
decorated with tiny hand
painted Venetian glass beads
which acted as weights. Lady
Diana Cooper recalls the
flattering way the dress hung:
'In every crude and subtle
colour, they clung like a
mermaid's scales.' When
removed, the dramatic effect
of the pleating mysteriously
disappeared and the dress
crumpled down to a small
heap of fabric.

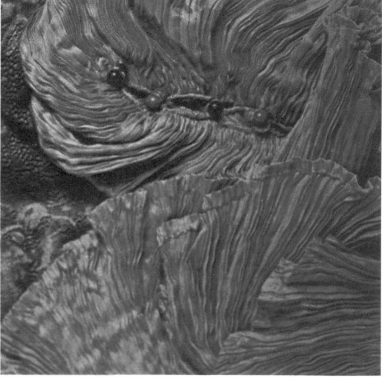

A drawing by Georges Barbier in 1917 of Isadora Duncan wearing a dress similar to Fortuny's Delphos. She was one of Fortuny's many famous clients.

the bronze statue of the Delphic charioteer, Fortuny saw his dress as an invention – he patented it in 1909, and throughout his life he made variations on it

He employed the finest Japanese, Chinese and Indian silks, which he coloured using mediaeval dye recipes to create rich mellow hues. Inspired by the Renaissance, he created dress from panels of velvet which fell to the ground at the back in a train. The sides were inset with pleated silk. Marcel Proust was inspired by this dress describing it as 'faithfully antique, but powerfully original.' Fortuny also made jackets, mantles and capes from rich velvets, all exquisitely decorated by hand using a stencil technique or hand painted in gold and silver. Each cloth was unique.

Marcel Proust evokes the splendour of Fortuny fabrics:

'The Fortuny gown that Albertine was wearing that evening seemed to me the tempting phantom of that invisible Venice. It swarmed with Arabic ornaments like the Venetian palaces, hidden like sultanas behind a screen of pierced stone, like the bindings in the Ambrosian library, like the columns from which the oriental birds that symbolize alternatively life and death, were repeated in the mirror of the fabric, of an intense blue which, as my gaze extended over it, was changed into a malleable gold, by those same transmutations which before the advancing gondolas, change into flaming metal the azure of the Grand Canal. And the sleeves were lined with a cherry pink, which is so peculiarly Venetian that it is called Tiepolo pink.'

Inspiration for Fortuny's textile designs came from his own extensive library which he inherited from his father and which he continued to add to. He made detailed studies of historic fabrics, of Renaissance painters, such as Jacopo Bellini and Carpaccio, and of oriental art.

His work was greatly admired and, as well as Marcel Proust, D'Annunzio was also inspired by his creations. Fortuny controlled both the production and marketing of his textiles and dress which took place at the Palazzo Orfei. In 1909 the ground floor of the Palazzo became a shop which sold original fabrics and dress and he established a network of international outlets. His dress was highly prized and sought after; Isadora Duncan, Sarah Bernhardt, the Countess Greffulhe, the Duchesse of Gremont, Queen Mary of Romania and Elenor Duse wore them, and others followed. Lady Diana Cooper recalls in her memoir *The Rainbow Comes and Goes*, her first sighting in 1907:

> 'Princess Murat, a fascinating surprise and totally different from anything we knew … wore the first of these tanagra-esque garments, later sold by thousands (many to me over twenty years) made by Fortuny of Venice – timeless dresses of pure thin silk cut severely straight from shoulder to toe, and kept wrung like a skein of wool. In every crude and subtle colour, they clung like mermaid's scales.'

They were initially worn as teagowns with tunics or gauze capes, and decorated with tiny Venetian glass beads, and it was not until the thirties that American women began wearing them to restaurants and the theatre.

Marcel Proust wrote in *The Captive*:

> 'In the matter of dress, what appealed to her most at this time was everything that was made by Fortuny. These Fortuny gowns, one of which I had seen Mme. de Guermantes wearing, were those of which Elstir, when he told us about the magnificent garments of the women of Carpaccio's and Titian's day, had prophesied the speedy return, rising from their ashes, sumptuous for everything must return in time, as it is written beneath the vaults of Saint Mark's, and proclaimed where they drink, from urns of marble and jaspar of the Byzantine capitals, by the birds which symbolize at once death and resurrection. As soon as women had begun to wear them, Albertine had remembered Elstir's prophecy, she had desired to have one and we were to go and choose it. Now these gowns, even if they were not those genuine antiques in which women today seem a little too much "in fancy dress" and which it is preferable to keep as pieces in a collection (I was in search of these also, as it happens for Albertine) could not be said to have the chilling effect of the artificial, the sham antique.'

After the First World War Fortuny recognized the need to diversify, and consequently in 1919 he established the Società Anonima Fortuny on the island of Giudecca, where he opened a print factory in a former Napoleonic prison. He created intricately decorated cottons intended for interiors, which he sold along with his silks and velvets in his Paris shop in Rue Charron next door to Poiret's Rosine boutique.

This kimono-type evening jacket is made of hand printed black silk velvet. The pattern, drawn from the Renaissance motifs Fortuny particularly favoured, is printed in metallic pigment. The jacket is edged with a different design of printed green velvet and lined with red silk and wool *faille*. It is worn with an elegant black satin Delphos evening dress (c. 1920). (Photograph: Victoria and Albert Museum).

The neckline of a Fortuny
dress, showing his label sewn
into the silk lining. The dress
is made of silk velvet in a rich
glowing colour. Each of these
dresses had unique hand
painted ornaments, in this
case of an oriental flavour.
Proust described them by
saying 'These gowns, even if
they were not genuine
antiques ... could not be said
to have the chilling effect of
the artificial, the sham
antique.'

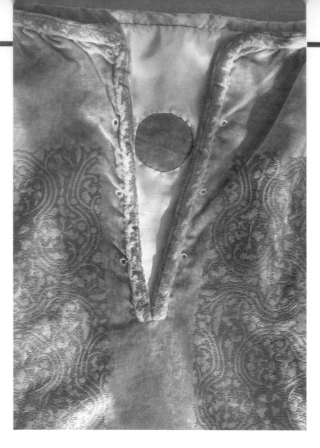

The cuff of a Fortuny
coat made in hand painted
velvet, featuring Renaissance
ornament.

'Whichever way one turns, one discovers nothing but over-hanging lengths of cloth, in very warm and subtle shades, enriched with magical ornamentation. It is really bewitching. One feels that some tale from *The Thousand and One Nights* is going to unfold against this decorative background, or perhaps some scene from Renaissance Venice.' (from *La Renaissance de l'Art Française des Industries de Luxe*, 1924)

Registering as a painter, Fortuny contributed to the Paris Exhibition in 1925 and showed his textiles and dress in both the Italian and Spanish sections.

Throughout the twenties and thirties, there was considerable demand for Fortuny dress. *Vogue* featured them, American cinema stars wore them. In 1936 the Italian government imposed a trade embargo in order to promote self sufficiency. Fortuny could no longer easily avail himself of the precious Japanese, Chinese and Indian silks he so desperately needed and consequently his output was considerably reduced. He died in 1949, and the Palazzo Orfei became the Palazzo Fortuny as a tribute to his life and work. His friend the Comtesse Gozzi still works there, executing the famous Fortuny fabrics.

A blouse made up of Fortuny fabric for Professor Randolf Schwaber, the principal of the Slade School of Art. The design, printed on a fine silk crêpe, dates from 1913 and features motifs from Cretan art.

SONIA DELAUNAY

A printed crêpe de Chine silk by Sonia Delaunay in 1926. She used cheap Japanese silks in order to make her clothes more widely accessible, but because they became so fashionable they remained expensive.

She applied her daring 'simultaneous' colour theories to fabric design, and ushered in the style of crisp lines and blocks of primary colours that took over from the heavily embossed fabrics of earlier Art Deco design.

Using her theories on simultaneous colours the artist Sonia Delaunay not only painted canvases, but extended her work to include household objects such as curtains, cushions, screens, carpets, tapestries, lampstands, lampshades, fabrics and fashion.

In collaboration with the couturier Jacques Heim, she exhibited at the International Exhibition of Decorative Arts in Paris in 1925. Her boutique Simultanée on Pont Alexander III, showed a range of her simultaneous designs executed in bold primary colours with a mathematical precision. With geometrical patterns for fabrics, screens, handbags and scarves, they were enthusiastically received.

Sonia Delaunay was born in 1885 in the Ukraine, of wealthy Russian parentage. She came to Europe to study art when she was twenty, spending two years in Germany before coming to Paris in 1905, where she studied at L'Academie de la Palette. In order to remain in Paris and to placate her parents, she made a marriage of convenience with Wilhelm Uhde, a German art dealer who was based there. The following year she divorced him to marry the Cubist painter Robert Delaunay. Their friends were part of the artistic and literary avant garde and included Braque, Apollinaire, Blaise Cendrars and Léger.

During the first years of her marriage, Sonia Delaunay together with her husband researched and developed their theories on colour, relating to form, space and movement, which they later named simultaneous colour. A patchwork quilt executed in the traditional Russian manner for the birth of her son Charles in 1909 'suggested to both artists new ideas about space and movement'. While other artists drew then coloured, Sonia Delaunay, who 'favoured colour, bearer of rhythm', drew with colour and created colour rhythms. By 1913 her painting, Bal Bullier, depicting the dancers at the Bullier dance hall epitomized her new style – blocks of colour were used in such a way as to show the angular movement of the dancers' bodies.

In 1913, Sonia Delaunay applied her new discoveries to illustration, and collaborated with the poet Blaise Cendrars to illustrate *Prose on the Trans-Siberian Railway*. She also became interested in applying her designs to household objects such as lampstands, lampshades and carpets. Using coloured pieces of cloth given to her by her husband's tailor, she constructed her first simultaneous dress which was to be the inspiration for others. The first sighting

Right: Sonia Delaunay with some of her early silks highlighting the element of movement in the fabric. Colour and movement were an integral part of her theories on fabric design.

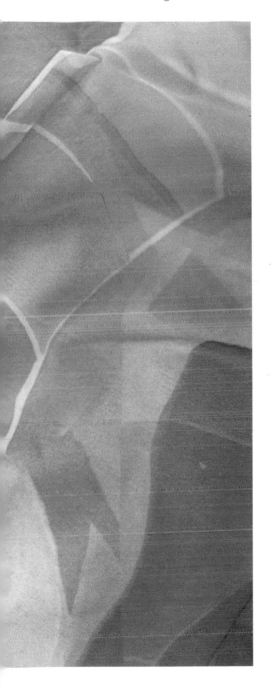

Below: A Delaunay fabric design from 1924–5, bought from her in 1967 for reproduction by Zika Ascher from the famous Ascher house in Wigmore Street.

of the dress, made up of small pieces of cloth in a harmonious whole, was at the Bal Bullier, the Delaunays' local nightclub which they frequented with friends each Thursday and Sunday night. Guillaume Apollinaire wrote in the 1 January 1914 edition of the *Mercure de France*:

'Monsieur and Madame Robert Delaunay have undertaken to reform costume. It is imperative to go to the Bullier and see what they are doing.

The innovation in the way of clothing brought about by simultaneous Orphism are not to be disregarded. These could have inspired a chapter in Carlyle's *Sartor Resartus*. The Delaunays are innovators. But in so far as they neither care for outworn fashions, nor seek to depart from the styles of their own times, their innovation lies in their desire to influence fashion through new textures and a great diversity of colours.

Take for example one of M. Robert Delaunay's costumes: purple jacket, beige waistcoat, dusky black trousers. Or this one: red coat with a blue collar, red socks, black and yellow shoes, green jacket, sky-blue waistcoat and, at last, a tiny red tie. To complete the picture, here is one of Mme. Delaunay's simultaneous dresses: a purple costume with a long purple and green belt, underneath a blouse which is divided into areas of different colours, bright, gentle or faded, intermingled with shades of salmon-pink, yellow-orange, powder-blue and scarlet. It is made up of juxtaposed fabrics of varying kinds such as taffeta, organdie, flannelette and pou-de-soie.

Such diversity has not passed unnoticed. She has combined fantasy with elegance.

And if you do happen to go to the Bullier, and if you do not manage to catch a glimpse of them straight away, know that these innovators have their place next to the orchestra. From this vantage point, they can contemplate, without the least scorn, the monotonous costumes of the dancers.'

These dresses were 'no longer pieces of material draped according to current fashion, but coherent compositions, living paintings or sculpture, using living forms.' They inspired Blaise Cendrars to write his poem *On her Dress she Wears a Body*.

The Delaunays spent the war years in Spain, and it was there that Sonia Delaunay began designing theatre costume, at first for the Madrid revue, and later for Diaghilev, and designed costumes for *Aïda* and *Cleopatra*. She used colour in such a way as to distort the body, and to give the impression of movement 'even before the dancer moved'.

Later in Paris, she collaborated with Tristan Tzara, the Dadaist poet, to create costumes for his play *Le Coeur à Gaz* which was performed as part of a Dadaist evening, with music by Satie, sets by Theo Van Doesburg and films by Man Ray.

Returning to Paris in 1921 without her income, as a consequence of the Russian Revolution, Sonia Delaunay devoted more time to illustration and applied arts through which she could earn a living. In

Delaunay fabric design, 1923.

1922 she executed some illustrations *Robes Poèmes* for Tristan Tzara's poetry; lines of verse were incorporated with geometrical blocks of colour in the shapes of dresses. A Lyons silk manufacturer noticed them and invited her to create a collection of fifty designs for fabrics. When they were released in 1923 they were highly acclaimed.

Consequently Delaunay continued designing and printing fabrics, and later opened a print workshop in order to supervise the work more closely. Her fabrics were used for wall hangings, furnishings and dress reaching a wide public and becoming very fashionable.

In the wake of Delaunay's simultaneous silks and designs, the ornate decorated fabrics which had been so popular before the war now appeared passé. Delaunay's simultaneous designs were copied, and became part of popular taste in the thirties. Delaunay opened an embroidery workshop, where Russian emigrés executed her geometrical designs in coloured wools for bags and coats – Gloria Swanson ordered one for her wedding trousseau. Working with Jacques Heim, the couturier, she designed swimwear, sportswear, handbags, coats and furs.

'Her luxurious coats in the gradation of colour found in autumn, or the delicate mists of morning, are fit to be worn by empresses,' wrote a contemporary, 'and she works fur in an

interesting personal manner, contrasting the subdued shades of skins with an astonishing virtuosity. She mingles fur and embroidery, metal threads with wool or silk, but only metal threads of a dull tone, achieving the effect of a rich and discreet elegance. She excels in all the accessories of the costume, hats, bags and belts reach an unsurpassable chic under her touch. Nothing could be more elegant in their quiet richness than her handbags embroidered in gold with a perfection of finish, comparable to that of jewellery. Everything she creates has the authentic touch of a true artist.'

Sonia Delaunay bridged the gap between fine and applied art by extending her art to a wide range of furnishings, dress and textiles, and she saw art as part of a popular tradition. By the 1930s Sonia Delaunay resumed her painting, although through her life she continued to design carpets and wall hangings.

Sonia Delaunay fashion designs, 1922–3. Her colourful geometric fabrics could be combined into highly original and striking garments, so that fashion design itself became an experiment in modern art.

CRTÉ

The Russian artist Erté is best known for his fashion designs and art illustrations, many of which appeared regularly in *Harper's Bazaar* between 1915 and 1938. Unlike other fashion artists Erté did not copy models, rather he created unique designs which provided inspiration to the fashion trade. He also made great contributions to theatre design, particularly to the Folies Bergères in Paris.

Erté was born Romain de Tirtoff in Saint Petersburg in 1892, the son of an Admiral of the Imperial Fleet, with a long line of descendants. Breaking with the family tradition, he left Russia in 1911 for Paris in order to pursue his interest in the arts and fashion. He studied painting at the Académie Julian, supporting himself by sending first-hand monthly reports and illustrations of Paris fashion to a Russian magazine, *The Ladies' World*. To avoid offending his family, he adopted the pseudonym 'Erté', which was derived from his initials RT pronounced in the French and Russian way 'Er-tay'. It was a name which was to become internationally known.

Erté in Monte Carlo in 1919 in provocative fancy dress. Erté worked for Poiret in the area of fancy dress, which was very popular with high society at the time.

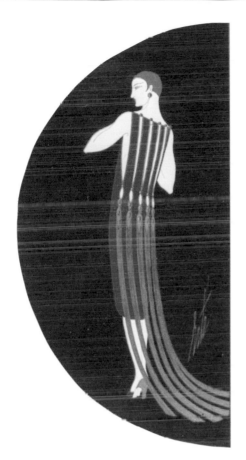

Costume design for the musical comedy *Manhattan Mary* produced in New York in 1927. Erté became deeply involved in the wider field of theatre and cinema designs, and designed for the Folies Bergères between 1917 and 1930. His paintings and drawings of his own fashion designs share the same fluid elegance as the costumes themselves.

In 1912, to supplement his income, Erté found a job working with a modiste called Caroline. Dismissing him after only one month, she told him that 'he should have nothing to do with design, a métier for which he had not the slightest gift.' Erté 'asked permission to take some of the designs I had done for her. She answered that she had thrown them all into the wastepaper basket, and I only had to empty it, which I did. I parcelled up the sketches and left them with Paul Poiret's porter.'

Poiret was very excited by this work, and in 1912 he invited Erté and his friend Zamorá to work with him as assistant designers. Erté designed coats, hats, headdresses and dress for the house.

La Maison Poiret as well as being a couture house had a theatrical workshop. It was run by Madame Régiane, who had worked with Landolff, the greatest theatrical costume designer of the day. Erté worked closely with Madame Régiane, designing theatrical and fancy dress. The fashion for lavish fancy dress parties was such that there was a great demand for original and fantastic costumes. Erté describes his own fancy dress, which he wore for the Grand Prix Bal at the Opéra, in the following way:

'I designed an oriental style costume for myself, in silver lamé. Closely moulded to the body, it had hundreds of strings of pearls linking the legs to the arms, and forming pearly wings. A pearl and silver helmet, crested with black plumes, and a black chiffon cape with a long, pearl embroidered train completed the ensemble. My arrival created a sensation.'

In 1913, collaborating with Poiret, he designed many of the costumes for Jacques Richepin's *Le Minaret*. Theatre design was to become an important aspect of his work, for productions such as George White's *Scandals*, for the opera, and for the Folies Bergères.

Erté's arrival in Paris coincided with a resurgence of interest in fashion illustration. Formerly used simply for the accurate depiction of dress, indicating each and every detail, it was soon to become a new art form. Whilst working with Poiret, Erté was invited to contribute some original designs to Lucien Vogel's luxury journal *Gazette du Bon Ton*, which was a 'show case in which only the most luxurious examples of high fashion, and the best of the decorative arts could be displayed, regardless of the cost involved'.

Erté contributed illustrations to magazines regularly.

'My work with Poiret soon led to another very important aspect of my art illustration. Poiret made me design models for reproduction in magazines, and for my black and white designs, I almost invariably used pen and Indian ink, although I later also used black and white gouache on a spread in tones of grey. My pen and ink technique developed rapidly, and became very precise, with extremely fine lines. I got to the point of using Gillot No. 3,000, the finest nib made.'

Inspiration for his work came from black and white Greek vase painting, and Persian and Indian miniatures.

In 1914, Erté left Paris for Monte Carlo, where for the next eight years, he was based at the Villa Excelsion. Erté continued designing sets and costumes for the theatre, and fashion for the American market. In 1914, he sent some designs to America to *Harper's Bazaar* and *Vogue*, and in 1916, Randolph Hearst from *Harper's Bazaar* offered him an exclusive ten year contract, which was subsequently renewed until 1938. During the first ten years, he designed the cover for each issue, he also designed fashion accessories, hats, bags, gloves, parasols, muffs, shoes, headdresses and interiors. These designs were imaginative, and created a distinctive style for the magazine.

Erté explained how he worked.

'I think that my case is unique among fashion artists. Usually there are illustrators who reproduce for magazines the models created by couturiers and dressmakers. I designed models of my own imagination without any precise objective. The result was that they became sources of inspiration for the fashion trade – yet they were designed as works of art … In designing dresses and coats, I thought first of all of the execution, above all the cut, as when I made a theatre decor, I thought first of the plan. I have always thought that a dress should be built almost like an architectural work, the conception can be either based on a length of material which, cut in a variety of ways becomes the form of the dress, or based on an amusing detail, around which the dress is designed.'

In 1924, Erté was invited to Hollywood to design costumes for Metro Goldwyn Mayer's films *Monte Carlo* and *Paris*. Together with his valet, and Nicolas his manager, he stopped in New York before boarding the luxury train, 'Twentieth Century Limited', which took four and a half days to cross the country to reach Los Angeles. Their arrival in Hollywood had been carefully prepared. MGM had built a reproduction of Erté's black and white Sèvres studio. Whilst in Hollywood, Erté cut an elegant figure, dressed in 'a gorgeous crimson and black brocaded coat over his pyjamas of pongee. The coat sumptuous and silken enough for an eastern potentate, was lined with cloth of gold, and sashed with the same. His pumps were inlaid with crimson leather.' He was fêted, and created great publicity for the studio.

Erté design for an evening dress for Poiret, drawn in pencil, pen and ink and gold. He worked with Poiret as head designer for dresses and hats, and developed an interest in fashion illustration.

Right: The Blue Angel
Musician costume (1926).
Erté's instinct for fantasy and
exotica gave him an
unequalled talent for lavish
theatrical costume design and
fancy dress.

Below: Design for an
Afternoon Dress, drawn in
pencil, with Indian ink and
water colour. The design
features the big flower motif
which was so widely popular
in fashion of the period.

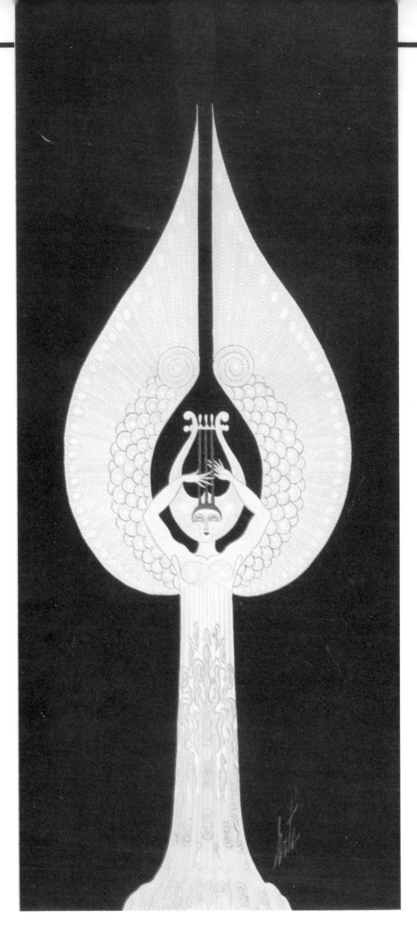

Above left: Erté was always invited to visit Hollywood when he went to the United States. This costume, designed in 1922, is for *The Seas.*

Above right: Carmel Myers as Iras, the vamp, in *Ben Hur* in 1925. The exotic headdress is typical of the Art Deco style.

Whilst working with MGM, Erté designed costumes for *Ben Hur*, and Aileen Pringle's costumes for *The Mystic.* His imaginative designs were ideally suited to film, which required costumes to be designed in such a way that they would not date for several years.

After nine months in Hollywood, Erté returned to Paris, where he has remained since the thirties, devoting most of his time to theatre design.

RAYMOND DUNCAN

The interest in classical antiquity in the late nineteenth century was reflected in the life and work of Raymond Duncan. He embraced two worlds, that of the ancient Greeks, and that of twentieth century Europe.

Raymond Duncan was born in 1878, of Irish-Scottish American stock. His sister, Isadora Duncan, was later to become the famous avant garde dancer. Their father, a one-time banker and newspaper proprietor, founded a school of decorative arts in San Francisco which involved his entire family. They became interested in the philosophies of the ancient Greeks, to such an extent that his mother and all her children left the United States in 1898 for Europe and Greece. A fellow passenger on the family's crossing was Gertrude Stein. She well remembered Raymond Duncan: 'He used to wear a carnation in his button hole and smoke cigars.' They travelled Europe visiting London, Berlin and Athens, where Isadora taught and perfected her free dance movements. While travelling from Brindisi to Athens they took a boat and requested the captain to re-route so as to follow the sea voyage of Ulysses, which he did.

Raymond spent five years in Greece, the first with the entire Duncan family while they acquainted themselves with the arts, crafts and theatre, and visited all the relics of classical antiquity. During this time, he and Isadora decided to adopt the dress of the ancient Greeks – a handwoven tunic, the shawl, and leather sandals – which Raymond wore for the rest of his life.

During his stay in Greece, Raymond and his wife Penelope set up a self-supporting community outside Athens based on the production of handspun and handwoven rugs designed by Raymond, and depicting various periods of Greek art. During World War I, he extended this, working with Turkish and Cypriot prisoners of war.

Despite frequent sojourns in the United States, Raymond Duncan settled in Paris and lived there till his death in 1966. In 1911 he founded a school for Greek arts and crafts in Paris where 900 students were taught the relevant aspects of his philosophy. This was based on the idea that the true value of work lies not in product or profit but in the development and growth of the worker. Classes included Greek tragedy, drama, dance movement, spinning, weaving and natural dyeing. Aia Bertrand attended his school in 1911 when she was sixteen. She was to become Duncan's life-long companion, and champion of his cause dedicating her life

A Duncan woodcut of Orpheus singing to the birds.

to his teachings. They lived collectively with a small group of followers in a colony in Neuilly, and kept to a vegetarian diet. Story has it that the colony supported a small herd of goats with bells, which could be seen in the early morning passing along the side streets in Paris on their way to be milked led by a goatherd complete with panpipes.

To finance all their projects, they created magnificently painted and brush-dyed silks depicting Greek gods, as well as hand-woven fabrics which were much prized by the fashionable.

Kaye Boyle, the American writer, and her daughter Sharon Walsh, joined the colony for a time in 1928. She recalls her first impressions of Raymond Duncan.

'He was a man of fifty or so, lean and muscular, neat and scrupulously well-kept, with his long hair pinned in silky braids in a crown around his small, eagle-like head. One end of his elegant tunic was flung across his left shoulder, and his bare feet, in the simplest of thonged sandals were immaculately clean.... He spoke with the flat twang of a midwest farmer, and his corded lean neck was that of a man who has worked in the fields or on the sea.'

The activities of the colony and school were complementary. To provide the necessary funds to support their activities and numerous projects, including printing, lithography, typography, hand spinning, Greek theatre, Socratic recitals and the like, they produced and sold exclusive printed silks. As chance would have it, these developed from Raymond's experiments to imitate coloured Greek head scarves. These provided the inspiration for silk tunics and panels which were hand-painted, or printed with hand-carved woodblocks. Border patterns were printed and a free-hand figure drawn on the centre celebrating Greek gods and myths. The

A detail of a brush-dyed Duncan silk, which was block printed and then hand painted with vegetable dyes.

outline was printed in with woodblocks and the vibrant colours made from natural dyes were painted in with a brush. This technique was called brush-dyeing. Members of the colony, including the children, assisted with the colouring. During the summer, when they left Paris, they continued this work in Nice, drying the fabrics on the beach. These silks were highly sought after and could be worn as capes, tunics and scarves. Wall hangings were also made, called 'Crepones', and were hand painted with figures of ancient Greece, sometimes with printed borders. Two boutiques were opened, decorated in Greek style with columns. One was on the Faubourg St Honoré and the other in St Germain. They sold handwoven carpets and leather sandals, and the assistants wore Greek dress. It was here that the young girls who were potential students for Elizabeth Duncan's 'Paris School of Greek Dance' were interviewed.

At the International Exhibition of Decorative Arts in 1925 Raymond Duncan was invited to exhibit. He built a huge wooden portico of a temple constructed in such a way that one could view simultaneously six paintings each 30 by 16 feet wide, and representing six parts of the world.

In 1929, Raymond Duncan moved his school and colony to the Rue de Seine which was later to become a museum for the four Duncans' work. After Raymond's death in 1966, at the age of 88, his companion Aia Bertrand continued to administer the museum until she died in 1980, at the age of 86.

Left: A drawing of Duncan's profile.

Below left: Aia Bertrand showing some of the collection of Duncan textiles from the Museum of Duncan in Paris.

Below right: Hand painted silk by Duncan celebrating the Greek heroic ideals by which he was deeply influenced.

UGO LO MONACO

Opposite: Lo Monaco specialized in extravagant, hand painted flowers and feathers – everything that could give an air of fantasy and finery to an outfit.

Some workshops such as Ugo Lo Monaco's not only designed and made embroideries, they also made lace and haute nouveauté – artificial flowers, hand-painted feathers, and de luxe decorations for dress. Lo Monaco set up his workshop in Rue Richelieu in 1906, initially learning his craft by buying and selling lace. His workshop comprised four sections – Embroidery, Lace, Feathers and Artificial Flowers – which were all created by highly skilled craftspeople. His work was in great demand, he had a large export trade and he worked closely with the leading couture establishments, as well as the theatre, lending his skills to the Russian Ballet. At the Exhibition of Decorative Arts in Paris in 1925, he was awarded a first prize for his work.

Artificial flowers such as roses, carnations, forget-me-nots, orchids, gardenia and violets were used both singly and as corsage to decorate dress, hats, bags and shoes. Lo Monaco supplied and created an extensive range of hand made natural and fantastic flowers made from fine silks, cottons, georgette, taffeta and ribbon. The petals for each flower were stamped between intricate metal moulds, cut out and hand painted in subtle gradations of colour before being mounted. Women excelled at this craft and some of them attended trade school. The workshop created sample ranges each season and the 'mounters' (women) assembled the orders in their own houses, many of which were in the provinces. Wages

Ugo Lo Monaco's card.

Broderies & Dentelles
HAUTE NOUVEAUTÉ

Ugo Lo Monaco

27. RUE RICHELIEU

TÉLÉPHONE
GUTENBERG 12·35

paris_1er

R.C.SEINE 404.888

*montre actuellement
la nouvelle Collection Broderies,
en Robes, Après-midi, Soir,
Sport, et Manteaux*

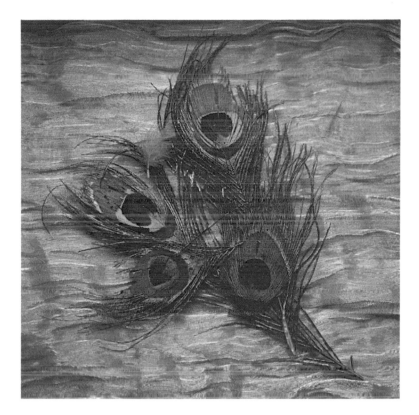

were low – for assembling leaves to wire stalks bound with green silk they were paid $1\frac{3}{4}$d to 2d (about 2 cents) per gross. This took one hour. A homeworker could earn five shillings to seven-and-six a week (about 10 cents), compared with thirteen shillings (75 cents) for an indoor worker.

Couturiers also availed themselves of the extensive range of hand-painted and decorated feathers used to embellish hats, day and evening dress. The lack of legislation to protect species of birds meant that cock, duck, swan, bird of paradise and pigeon plumage were decorated and hand-painted in vivid colours – flame orange, vivid green, black and white specks. When used by couturiers, they were applied to cloth of gold, brocade and silk and looked ravishing. Long green feather tips were beaded with pink glass. The Russian Ballet, and theatrical companies often incorporated these feathers in their costumes.

Lo Monaco designed and made embroideries for fashion, for day, afternoon, evening and sports dress as well as for coats. Each year he visited major museums and textile collections for inspiration. He based collections on particular themes such as Persian tiles, oriental rugs, Chinese ornaments or Coptic weaves, and he copied Indian jewellery, necklaces and bracelets in hand embroidery. His designs were refined and elegant, detailed and inventive, and, by comparison with La Maison Lallement's work, they were classical and restrained.

A page from one of Lo Monaco's sample books, showing a piece of embroidery which repeats the feathers theme. It is worked in brilliantly coloured silks on a very fine ground.

Besides Lo Monaco, another specialist embroidery house was the famous Kitmar Workshop. As a result of the Russian Revolution of 1917, aristocratic emigrés settled in Paris. They were forced to find a way of earning a living, many of them for the first time. Marie, Grand Duchess of Russia, made use of the only commercial skill she had – that of fine needlework which she had learnt as a child from nuns. She established her own workshop called Kitmar which specialized in machine embroidery. By 1925 it employed fifty women, many of them compatriots, who made original embroideries for couture. For several years they worked exclusively for Chanel, before working for other houses.

Another partly worked embroidery sample, that would probably have been incorporated into a dress. The design has been drawn out onto a lightweight crêpe de Chine, then hand embroidered with coloured silks and outlined in diamante sequins. Pretty and elegant, the style of the Lo Monaco embroideries is very distinct in character from those of the Atelier Martine or La Maison Lallement.

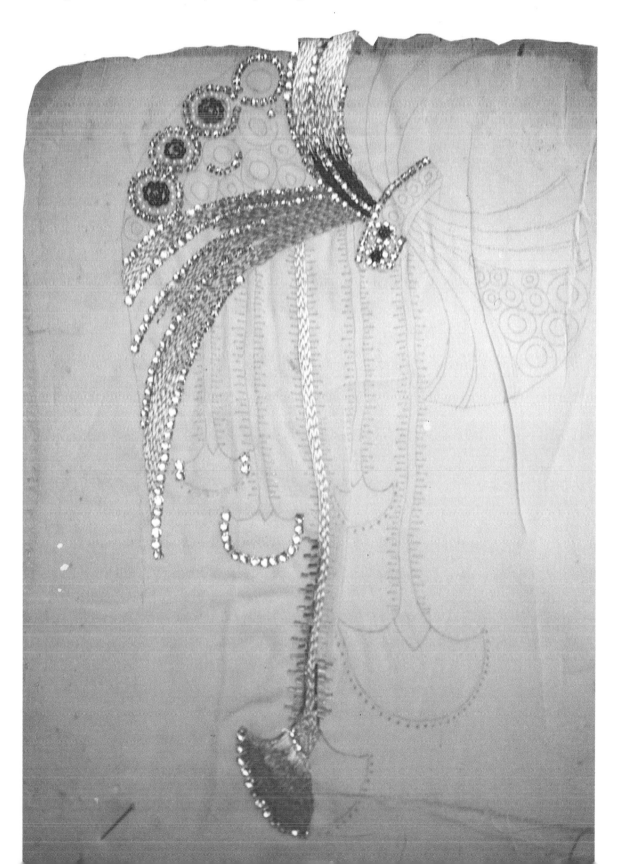

Left: A half embroidered and half drawn sample for a dress. The piece combines two grounds in different weights, hand embroidered. The centres of the flowers are filled with tiny gold beads, highlighted with gold and silver threads.

Below: Another partially worked sample embroidery in a design that is partly stylized to form a geometrical pattern, and partly reflects the form of overlapping feathers or scales. The design is drawn out, and worked in braids and embroidery on an ivory silk ground.

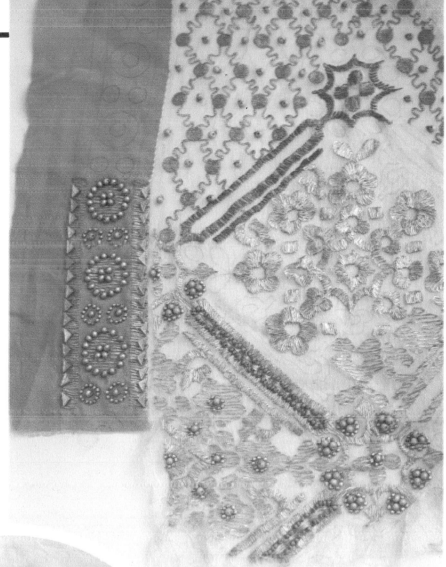

Pieces of beaded embroidery in the delicate colours and intricate patterns typical of Lo Monaco's work. Blue silk combined with lightweight silk chiffon, embroidered with metallic threads and beaded in blue and silver. The delicate filigree has been photographed against a yellow background.

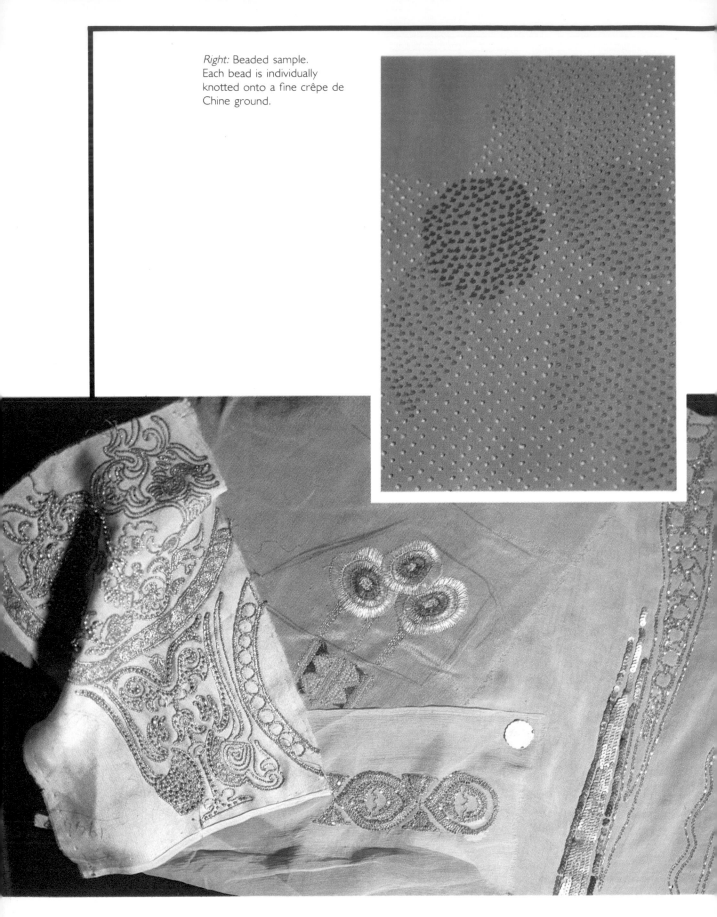

Right: Beaded sample. Each bead is individually knotted onto a fine crêpe de Chine ground.

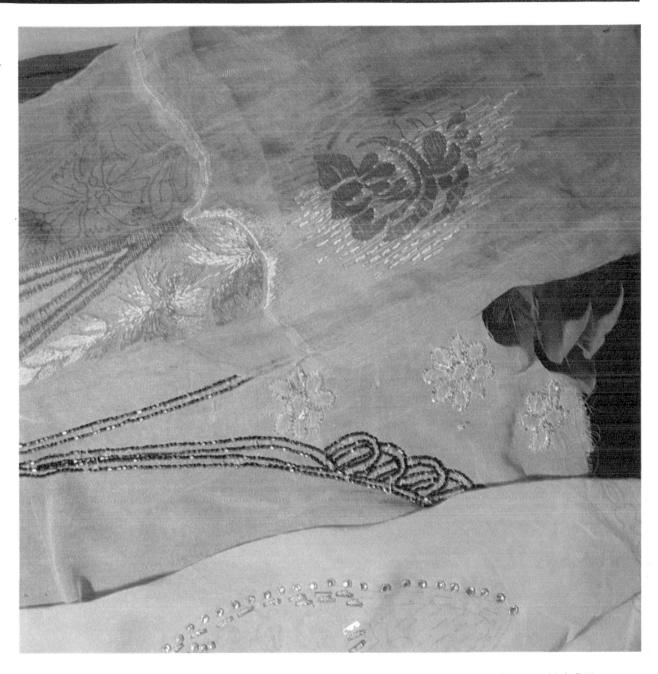

Above and left: Different samples of Lo Monaco's work.

FASHION ACCESSORIES

In 1920, Paris was the established centre for the luxury goods industry, with a revenue of 100 million francs from a thriving export trade in the year 1924.

Specialist craft workshops practising time-honoured and highly respected skills, made hats, bags, gloves and shoes – the essential and integral part of a woman's wardrobe – which were designed especially for each and every outfit. It was not unusual for a fashionable woman to have a truly vast selection of hats, bags, gloves and shoes, which were cared for by her personal maid who became the recipient of her last season's dress, too luxurious to wear. They were then sold, creating a thriving second, third and fourth hand clothing trade. By the 1920s accessories could be ordered from an individual couture house, individually designed and intricately decorated. Ready made accessories were obtainable from department stores. At the Paris Exhibition, cordonniers, umbrella makers, glove and bag makers displayed their work in a section devoted to parure (accessories). The resulting fashion fantasies, were achieved by collaboration between creative artists and the manufacturers, independent artists, couturiers, seam-stresses and shoemakers.

BAGS

By 1925, dress was, to quote Colette in *Vogue*, 'Short, flat, geometrical and quadrangular. Feminine wear is fixed along the line of the parallelogram. And 1925 shall not see the comeback of soft curves, arrogant breasts and enticing hips'. In order not to detract from this line, bags became small and compact, envelope or oval shaped, and were carried under the arm. They were intricately and inventively decorated.

'Every woman wants more than one bag, she wants a useful marketing and shopping bag, dainty theatre and tiny vanity bags for going out with, she would like one to match every costume.' Day bags harmonized with the hat and umbrella, evening bags harmonized with the dress. Skilled leather workers, such as Madame Claussen-Smith, made bags from fine leather, hand-dyed in vibrant colours and embossed and decorated with leather appliqué work or interwoven with leather strips. Some were made from exotic skins — shark, suede, snake. The bags were always large enough for women to carry their powder compacts and cigarette holders, which were luxury items in themselves. Iris Storm kept her powder in a 'hexagonal black onyx box, initialled in minute diamond letters, and chained to a cigarette case of white jade.'

The demand for cloth bags, which had developed during the War due to leather scarcity, continued. They were made by

Three Lallement bag designs, drawn onto a page in a workbook, accompanied by a sample of the embroidery. Each design was numbered and the details of the costings were set out alongside it.

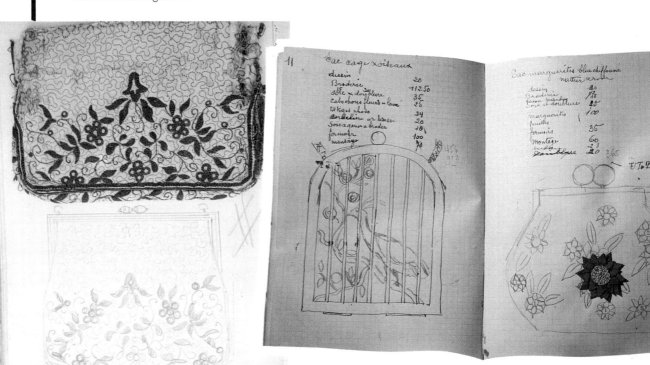

A partly worked sample for an evening bag. The ground is covered in French knots with leaves made from ribbon. The flower petals show an early experiment with appliquéd synthetic materials in fashion accessories.

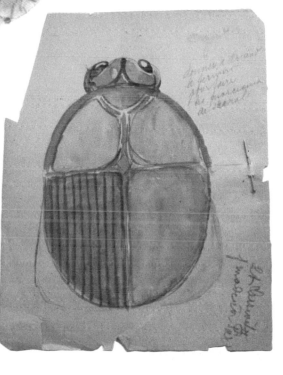

Right: A witty bag design for La Maison Lallement.

Drawing and embroidered sample for a bag decorated with a reindeer. The drawing shows a tassel hanging from beneath the bag.

specialist workshops, using luxurious fabrics, cloth of gold, brocades, silks, velvets. They were decorated and embroidered with cubist, aztec and sporting designs. Futurist bags were lined in silks and rayons in startling colours and some of the most splendid evening bags were completely hand-beaded.

A written note alongside these sketches describes them as 'futurist' bags.

A sample for a
Lallement embroidered bag,
with silver sequins on a pink
velvet ground.

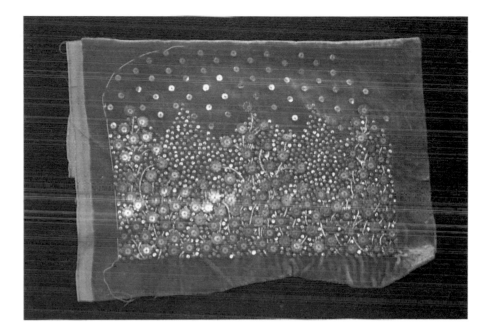

A design by Madame
Claussen Smith, a highly
skilled designer who used
leather in elegant patterns
dyed with strong colours.
Her designs were applied to
interior design as well as to
fashion accessories.

A shoe from The Costume Museum at Worthing. It is made of printed velvet with a heel shape and softly pointed toe typical of the 1920 period.

SHOES

Shoes were often made to order to complement particular outfits. They were worn with real or artificial silk stockings, many of which had a geometrical knitted openwork pattern on the side of the leg. Shoes had the popular Louis XV two-inch heel and rounded toes, and leather ones, in crocodile, buckskin or kid, were decorated with metal and enamel buckles. It was not uncommon for shoes to be made from the same fabric as the dress.

An Erté glove design.

GLOVES

Hand-made gloves were an essential requisite for fashionable women. Stored in ivory boxes with ivory or ebony stretchers they were worn for most occasions, since despite a greater informality in dress an etiquette still persisted. Gloves were made from fine leathers, kid and suede in pastel colours, they were also worn in grey, black, white or rose to match silk stockings. Gloves were cut with a gauntlet, and were embroidered with silks, chenille and beadwork in floral geometric designs, some inspired by Slavic or Russian folk art. The points of gloves were stitched or inset with leather appliqué work in contrasting colours, executed by glovers, many of whom trained at the glove decoration school in Grenoble. Small leather purses were attached by a silken cord to the gauntlet.

HATS

The cloche hat was the success of the twenties. Small, smooth and closely fitted to the head, it epitomized the streamlined machine age that had begun to excite artists such as Léger. Milliners skillfully and inventively moulded felts, folding the surplus material to the one side of the head and decorating it with flowers and feathers, others were pinned with platinum and diamonds.

A cloche hat by Marthe Callot from *La Gazette du Bon Ton.*

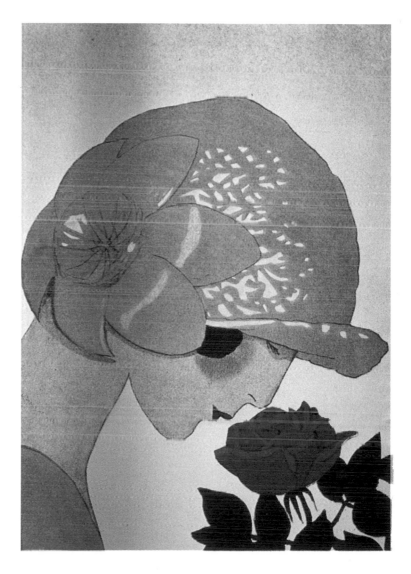

A typical close fitting
1920s evening hat made in
silver lamé from the Antique
Costume and Textile Gallery
in London. It would have
been worn throughout the
evening as an integral part of
the costume.

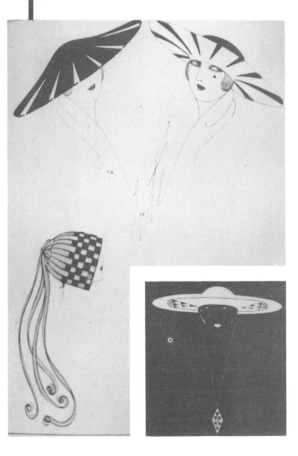

Opposite: A page from
Needle-Art magazine, Spring
1922, headed 'Charming
Flowers of Silk and Ribbon.'
Instructions on making the
flowers are given elsewhere
in the magazine.

Left: Erté hat designs.

CHARMING FLOWERS OF SILK AND RIBBON

(For directions see page 24)

BIBLIOGRAPHY

POIRET

En Habillant L'Epoque. Paul Poiret. Grasset, 1931.
Poiret le Magnifique. Preface by Julien Cain. Musée Jaquemart, Paris, 1974.
Poiret. Academy Editions, 1979.
My First Fifty Years. Paul Poiret, translated by Stephen Haden-Guest. Victor Gollancz, 1931.
Poiret. Palmer White. Studio Vista, 1973.

DUFY

Raoul Dufy, Création d'Etoffes. Jean-Michel Tushscherer. Musée de L'Impression sur Etoffes de Mulhouse, 1973.
Raoul Dufy, 1877–1953. Arts Council of Great Britain, 1983.

FORTUNY

Mariano Fortuny, His Life and Work. Guillermo de Osma. Arum Press, 1980.

SONIA DELAUNAY

Sonia Delaunay. Art Curial. Centre d'Art Plastique Contemporain, Paris.
Sonia Delaunay and the Expanding Definiton of Art. Claire Rendell. Women's Art Journal, Spring 1985.
Sonia Delaunay. Jacques Damase. Galerie de Varrene, Paris, 1971.
Robes et Gouaches Simultanées, 1925. Jacques Damase. L'Art et le Corps Rythmés – Couleurs en Mouvement, Paris, 1975.

ERTÉ

Things I Remember, An Autobiography. Peter Owen, London, 1975.
Erté. Charles Spencer. Studio Vista, 1972.

RAYMOND DUNCAN

Exangelos. Raymond Duncan. French Edition, Paris, Editorial no. 265, January 1976.

UGO LO MONACO

The Princess in Exile – Marie Grand Duchess of Russia. Cassell, 1932.

GENERAL BACKGROUND

My Life. Isadora Duncan. Victor Gollancz, London, 1974.
An Impression of Angels, A Biography of Jean Cocteau. Frederick Brown. Longman, 1968.
The Rainbow Comes and Goes. Lady Diana Cooper. Rupert Hart-Davis, 1958.
Being Geniuses Together, 1920–1930. Robert Mcalmon and Kay Boyle. Hogarth Press, 1984.
In Search of Diaghilev. Richard Buckle. New York, 1956.
Marcel Proust and His Time. Wildenstein Gallery, London, 1955.

FASHION

Into the Twenties: Style and Design, 1909–1929. Thames and Hudson, London, 1968. Also published as *Style and Design, 1909–1929.* Brazillen, New York, 1968.
Paris à La Mode, A Voyage of Discovery. Celia Berton. Victor Gollancz, London, 1956.
Paris Fashion. Edited by Lynam Roth. Michael Joseph, London, 1972. Clarkson Potter, New York, 1972.
The Cut of Women's Clothes, 1600–1930. N. Waugh. Faber and Faber, London, 1968.
The Decorative Twenties. Martin Battersby. Studio Vista, 1969.
Gloves. Valerie Cumming. Batsford, 1982.
Bags and Purses. Vanda Foster. Batsford, 1982.
Hats. Fiona Clark. Batsford, 1982.
Art Deco Catalogues (facsimile). Garland, New York.
Fashion 1900–1939. Arts Council. Victoria and Albert Museum, 1974.
Twentieth Century Embroidery in Great Britain, 1900–1939. Constance Howard. Batsford, 1985.
Machine Embroidery, a Complete Guide. Christine Risley. Studio Vista, 1983.
Fashion Revivals From the Elizabethan Age to the Present Day. Barbara Burman Baines. Batsford, 1981.
In Fashion: Dress in the Twentieth Century. Prudence Glynn with Madeleine Ginsburg. Allen and Unwin, 1978.
Married Women's Work. Clementina Black. Virago reprint, 1984.
The Subversive Stitch – Embroidery and the Making of the Feminine. Roziska Parker. The Women's Press, 1984.
A Woman's Touch – Women in Design from 1860 to the Present Day. Isabelle Anscombe. Virago, 1984.
The Collector's Book of Twentieth Century Fashion. Frances Kennett. Granada, 1983.
400 Years of Fashion. Victoria and Albert Museum/Collins, 1984.
History of Twentieth Century Fashion. Ewing. Batsford, 1974.

PERIODICALS

Vogue, 1916–1930.
Costume Journal number 12, 1978: Millinery Techniques in the 1920s.
Gazette du Bon Ton, 1913–14, 1920–25.

ACKNOWLEDGEMENTS

So many people have helped both directly and indirectly over the years in the completion of this project.

I would like to thank everyone, especially Suzanne Lallement, Jean Dorville, Ugo Lo Monaco, Jane Raphane, Arletty, Madame Chesnais, Phillipe Chabenix, Madame Chabenix, Alice Natter, Margarette Gallot, Aia Bertrand, Sonia Delaunay, Jean-Michel Tushscherer, Madame Claussen-Smith, Isobel Bedat, Ligoua Duncan. Marion Nichols, Valerie White (Fashion Librarian, North East London Polytechnic), Judith Preece (Art Librarian, North East London Polytechnic), the fashion design and marketing staff and students of North East London Polytechnic, and the textile students from Loughborough College of Art and Design, who encouraged and supported my work, Stella Mary Newton, Karen Finch, Eva Louise Svenson, Claire Rendell, Gillian Elenor, Elizabeth Astbury, Rosie Edwards, Nanda and Chris Coolsma, David and Renab Henning, James Mollison (Director of the Australian National Gallery Canberra), the Australian Crafts Board, Valerie Mendes. (The Victoria and Albert Museum), Anna Bowman, Penny Radford, Isobel Vicontesse D'Orthez, Anne George (Senior Assistant Librarian, Royal College of Art), Souki Tomas, Philippa Frances-Scot, The Gallery of Antique Costume (London), Alyson Segal, Lionel Segal, Melanie Leach, Kate Buckley, Anne Higgins, Fiona Pink (Worthing Costume Museum), Angela Williams (St John's College, Oxford), Dr Penny and Robert Gay, Francoise Undacath, Elizabeth Brooke-Smith.

ILLUSTRATION
ACKNOWLEDGEMENTS

All the photographs are by Michel Molinare except:
p.15 (top), p.19, pp.20–21, p.22 (below), p.23, p.25, p.29, pp.46–55, p.61 (below), p.72, p.78, p.81, p.83, pp.85–97, p.118 (below), p.119, p.120 (left) and p.121.

The publishers would like to thank the following:
Photographs on p.13 (both), p.112, p.120 (top): The Antique Costume Gallery, London.
Photographs on p.19, p.21, p.25: Collection de Wilde Poiret.
Photograph on p.22: reproduced from *Poiret*, published by Academy Editions, 1979. © DACS 1985.
Photographs on p.23, pp.50–51 (top), p.54, p.83, pp.90 91 (b/ws), p.95, p.96 (left): reproduced by courtesy of the Board of Trustees of the Victoria and Albert Museum.
Photograph on p.24: Souki Tomas.
Photographs on p.46, p.48 (top), p.49 (left), pp.50–51 (top), p.51 (below), p.52, p.53, p.54, p.55: © DACS 1985.
Photographs on p.48 (top), p.51 (below), p.52, p.53, p.55, p.86: The Musée Historique des Tissus, Lyon.
Photograph on p.49 (right): Helmut Newton.
Photograph on p.79: Philippa Frances.
Photograph on p.85: Glasgow Museums and Art Galleries – Camphill House Museum of Costume.
Photograph on p.86, p.88 (both), pp.90 91: © ADAGP 1985.
Photographs on pp.92–97, p.118 (below), p.120 (below): reproduced from *Things I Remember, An Autobiography*, published by Peter Owen Ltd, London, 1975. © Sevenarts Limited London.
Photograph on p.118 (top): Costume Museum, Worthing.
Drawing on p.81 and cover: Miss H. Fritz-Denneville.
Photographs on p.29 (top) and p.48 (right): Photo Lipnitzki-Viollet.

The quotations in the Erté chapter from *Things I Remember, An Autobiography* are reproduced with the kind permission of Peter Owen Ltd.